EGGS

Edible

Series Editor: Andrew F. Smith

EDIBLE is a revolutionary series of books dedicated to food and drink that explores the rich history of cuisine. Each book reveals the global history and culture of one type of food or beverage.

Already published

Apple Erika Janik *Barbecue* Jonathan Deutsch and Megan J. Elias *Beef* Lorna Piatti-Farnell *Beer* Gavin D. Smith *Bread* William Rubel *Cake* Nicola Humble *Caviar* Nichola Fletcher *Champagne* Becky Sue Epstein *Cheese* Andrew Dalby *Chocolate* Sarah Moss and Alexander Badenoch *Cocktails* Joseph M. Carlin *Curry* Colleen Taylor Sen *Dates* Nawal Nasrallah *Eggs* Diane Toops *Game* Paula Young Lee *Gin* Lesley Jacobs Solmonson *Hamburger* Andrew F. Smith *Herbs* Gary Allen *Hot Dog* Bruce Kraig *Ice Cream* Laura B. Weiss *Lemon* Toby Sonneman *Lobster* Elisabeth Townsend *Milk* Hannah Velten *Mushroom* Cynthia D. Bertelsen *Nuts* Ken Albala *Offal* Nina Edwards *Olive* Fabrizia Lanza *Oranges* Clarissa Hyman *Pancake* Ken Albala *Pie* Janet Clarkson *Pineapple* Kaori O' Connor *Pizza* Carol Helstosky *Pork* Katharine M. Rogers *Potato* Andrew F. Smith *Rum* Richard Foss *Salmon* Nicolaas Mink *Sandwich* Bee Wilson *Soup* Janet Clarkson *Spices* Fred Czarra *Tea* Helen Saberi *Whiskey* Kevin R. Kosar *Wine* Marc Millon

Eggs

A Global History

Diane Toops

REAKTION BOOKS

For my son Phillip and my grandson Templar Toops

Published by Reaktion Books Ltd
33 Great Sutton Street
London EC1V 0DX, UK
www.reaktionbooks.co.uk

First published 2014

Printed and bound in China
by Toppan Printing Co. Ltd

A catalogue record for this book is available
from the British Library

ISBN 978 1 78023 264 5

Contents

Introduction: Walking on Eggs

A day without an argument is like an egg without salt.

Angela Carter

Fascination with the perfect symmetry, beauty, functionality and mysterious symbolism of the egg has existed since time immemorial. It represents the beginning of time, a source of life, wisdom, strength, vitality, procreation, death and Christ's reincarnation, bound together by tales of the creation of the world and man from an egg, summed up in the Latin proverb *omne vivum ec ovo* (all life comes from the egg). In legendary accounts it is often an egg that floats on water and is the source of all things. The American folklorist Zora Neale Hurston (1891–1960) succinctly declared, 'The present was an egg laid by the past that had the future inside its shell.' One notable image of the egg as a source of all things is an eighteenth-century engraving of an alchemist trying to get wisdom and knowledge, or 'that Elixir by which wonders are performed', out of the egg-shaped philosopher's stone, demonstrating the reverence in which the egg was held. Although he used both fire and sword, he did not annihilate the egg completely, so that it could grow and receive new life.

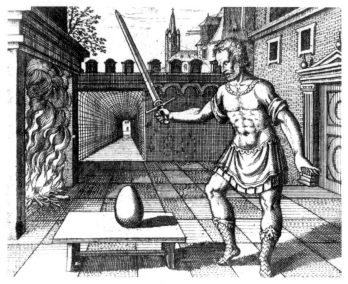

The Philosopher's Egg, or the egg as the source of all things, 18th century, engraving.

'To the Chinese, the egg is more than a versatile food', according to chef Martin Yan.

> It's an important cultural symbol, thought to embody not only the beginning of the life cycle, but also the wholeness of yin (white represents bright, male energy and heaven) and yang (yolk represents dark, female energy and earth) held together in a circle (shell represents creation). The joining of yin and yang creates a balance of wisdom, truth, purity, propriety and kindness, making the egg the 'food of five virtues'.[1]

However, it is not only the mystery of the egg's connection to our universe that captivates us; it is the magical qualities it brings to cooking. 'You begin with a slippery, runny liquid, do nothing more than add heat, and presto: The liquid rapidly stiffens into a solid that you can cut with a knife,' writes food scientist Harold McGee.[2] 'No other ingredient is as readily and drastically transformed as is the egg.'

For some an egg is just an egg, an all-natural, delicious, inexpensive, protein-rich food that can be eaten alone or used as an ingredient in a recipe, and the chances are that one is readily available in your refrigerator. There is no doubt that an egg is truly the most valuable player in the home kitchen. Even the most cooking impaired can use eggs to provide sustenance for their family for breakfast, lunch or dinner, or as a snack. Not surprisingly, 94 per cent of all households in the United States use eggs, averaging 33 eggs per month, or 396 each year per household. According to a 2011 Mintel survey, regular white eggs are most popular with 88 per cent of respondents, brown eggs are favoured by 27 per cent, organic eggs are the first choice of 27 per cent and 14 per cent prefer free-range eggs.

Eggs Benedict: eggs transformed from raw to poached, and to an ingredient in hollandaise sauce.

But 30 per cent eat fewer eggs than they once did because of concerns about cholesterol, and 57 per cent do not believe that organic eggs are any healthier than regular eggs.

Eggs Scramble for Respectability

Eggs have received an inordinate amount of bad press and have taken a lot of heat in the past few decades as to their healthfulness. When the final version of *Dietary Goals for the United States*, a report prepared by the Senate Select Committee on Nutrition and Human Needs, was released in 1977 with much fanfare,[3] it targeted eggs and other foods 'high in saturated fats and cholesterol', recommending that Americans cut their egg consumption by 50 per cent to prevent elevated cholesterol levels and the increased risk of heart disease. The American Medical Association disagreed with the report, stating that there was not enough evidence to support the committee's findings.

Walking on eggshells, so to speak, consumers feared dietary cholesterol and chose to pay attention to the government's warning by restricting their egg intake, purchasing fewer eggs. However, only the yolk contains cholesterol (213 milligrams at that time), so food manufacturers were challenged to develop cholesterol-free eggs to encourage consumption. Formulations using egg whites that could be scrambled or used in baking were developed. They consist of genuine egg whites mixed with an imitation of the yolk, and are usually made from vegetable oil, milk solids and gums that provide a thick consistency, as well as colourings, flavourings, and vitamin and mineral supplements. Then came results from long-term scientific studies, one after another, proving that scientists had erred. Nutrients in eggs actually reduce the risk of inflammation

The nutritional
content of eggs.

Nutrition Facts
Serving Size Large Egg (50 g)
Servings per container 1

Amount Per Serving

Calories 71	Calories from Fat 45
	% Daily Value*
Total Fat 5g	8%
Saturated Fat 2g	8%
Trans Fat	
Cholesterol 211mg	70%
Sodium 70mg	3%
Total Carbohydrate 0g	0%
Dietary Fiber 0g	0%
Sugars 0g	
Protein 6g	
Vitamin A 6% • Vitamin C	0%
Calcium 3% • Iron	5%

*Percent Daily Values are based on a 2,000 calorie diet. Your daily values may be higher or lower depending on your calorie needs.

associated with chronic diseases such as heart disease, bone
loss, dementia and Alzheimer's disease. Saturated fat is a much
bigger problem than dietary cholesterol. A large egg contains
only 1.5 g of saturated fat, a relatively small amount. After more
than 40 years of research, eggs were redeemed. 'I have long
suspected that eliminating eggs from the diet generally has the
opposite effect,' said Dr David Katz, director of the Yale
University Prevention Research Center. 'In our own studies of
egg intake, we have seen no harmful effects, even in people
with high blood cholesterol.'

By law, the U.S. Department of Agriculture (USDA) and the
U.S. Department of Health and Human Services (HHS) must
review, update if necessary and publish the *Dietary Guidelines for*

Americans every five years.[4] Based on the Dietary Guidelines Advisory Committee's report and public comments, the 2010 guidelines recommended that Americans consume a variety of protein foods – seafood, lean meat and poultry, beans and peas, soy products, unsalted nuts and seeds, and eggs. New USDA data found that the cholesterol content of eggs had dropped significantly since 2002 levels, as the result of nutritional improvements in carefully balanced poultry feed made up of corn, soy-bean meal, cotton-seed meal, or sorghum, with added vitamins and minerals. According to the USDA, the cholesterol in one large egg – or its 50 g (1¾ oz) equivalent within the further processed egg ingredient category – is 12 per cent lower at 185 milligrams, and also contains 41 IU of vitamin D, an increase of 64 per cent.[5]

Eggs hatched a comeback, and most nutritionists and doctors agree that eggs are an excellent protein source and do not raise levels of low-density lipoprotein (LDL, or 'bad') cholesterol. This conclusion led to renewed interest and greater consumption of eggs, particularly in China and the United States, two countries with populations that suffer from both LDL cholesterol and obesity. And although Gaston from the Disney film *Beauty and the Beast* (1991) boasts that, 'Now that I'm grown, I eat five dozen eggs, so I'm roughly the size of a barge!', new studies have determined that adults who eat two eggs a day actually lose weight. The protein keeps you fuelled and feeling satisfied, thus helping you to avoid further cravings.

Safe or Sorry

Egg nutrition has recently taken a back seat to food-safety scares. Recalls occur from time to time, but eggs have escaped relatively unscathed, other than in food-service prepared foods or at home, where people do not follow safe procedures or continue to eat uncooked biscuit dough made with raw eggs. No matter how tempting, eating uncooked eggs is dangerous, and should be avoided.

U.S. senators were left with egg on their faces in August 2010, when one of the great ironies in the history of food safety arose. A *Salmonella enteritidis* (SE) outbreak and the recall of half a billion eggs from Iowa farms occurred just as newly adopted, more stringent egg-safety rules were enacted. Salmonella testing of hens and eggs, better hen-house sanitation and improved refrigeration regulations had languished through 20 years of turf battles between the USDA and the U.S. Food and Drug Administration (FDA), which both regulate eggs. The USDA is responsible for live chickens and breaker plants/egg products processing facilities (where eggs are broken and pasteurized), while the FDA regulates shell eggs and egg products once they leave the breaking facility.

These new rules were enacted on major egg producers with the goal of cutting egg-related salmonella cases by 60 per cent, but required passage of an amendment to update the broader food-safety system by giving greater authority to regulators to police food manufacturers. Therein lies the crack in food-safety authority. Backlash from the egg recall led to the passage of the FDA Food Safety Modernization Act (FSMA), signed into law by President Barack Obama on 4 January 2011. The biggest overhaul of food-safety oversight in 70 years, the FSMA expanded the FDA's authority to order mandatory recalls, strengthen inspections of food processors and introduce tougher standards of safety on producers.

Problems with egg safety also occurred in Europe right before Christmas 2010. Oil intended for biofuels was mistakenly shipped to feed manufacturers earlier in the year, and 3,000 tons of contaminated animal feed reached 1,000 poultry and pig farms across Germany. Those contaminated eggs were sent to the Netherlands to be liquefied and pasteurized, and 14 tons of liquid eggs were sent to the United Kingdom and used in short shelf-life baked goods provided to a variety of retailers. Fortunately disaster was averted when the products were withdrawn, even though the danger was extremely low because the German eggs were mixed with uncontaminated eggs in Holland, diluting the dioxin before the eggs were shipped to the United Kingdom, according to the Food Standards Agency.

More recently, the issue for U.S. egg producers has been animal welfare. McDonald's, which conducted a three-year study comparing traditional cage-free and enriched laying

Eggs in a basket.

hen-housing systems on a commercial scale, buys one million cage-free eggs in the u.s. every month, but most of its eggs come from caged hens. In November 2011 an undercover video by animal rights activists showed some hens and chicks being mistreated and crowded into wire cages, and unsanitary conditions. Immediately McDonald's, followed by Target Corp, scrambled to sever ties with one of the major egg providers to McDonald's and many supermarket chains.

Beyond the Plate

Aside from being a food, the egg inadvertently saves lives. The small-scale apparatus for hatching eggs inspired the invention of incubators, which provide an environment of controlled heat, humidity and ventilation for prematurely born infants, as well as another type of incubator developed for the culture of micro-organisms. For centuries in China, India and Eastern Europe, eggs have been used as the base of health potions. Scientists today use lysozyme, an egg-white protein, as a food preservative and an antimicrobial agent in pharmaceutical products. Egg-white proteins avidin and biotin are useful in medical diagnostic applications such as immuno-assay, histo-pathology and gene probes. Sialic acid inhibits certain stomach infections, while liposomes, fatty droplets found in eggs, are used to model controlled delivery mechanisms for drugs. Immunoglobulin yolk, a simple egg-yolk protein, is used as a human-rotavirus (HRV) antibody, and phosvitin, a phospho-protein in egg yolk, provides antioxidant benefits in food products. Choline, a B-complex vitamin combined with lecithin in egg yolk, is important in brain development and is used to treat certain liver disorders. Ovolecithin, a phospholipid found in yolk, has a high proportion of phosphatidycholine and contains fatty acids – such as arachidonic acid (AA) and docosahexaenoic acid (DHA) – which improve visual acuity in infants. Egg lecithin has both emulsifying and antioxidant properties, and beyond its usefulness in keeping the oil and vinegar of mayonnaise in suspension, it is used in medicines for the same purpose. Shell-membrane protein is being used experimentally to grow human skin fibroblasts (connective tissue cells) for severe-burn victims.

In Japan, the shell membrane protein is used in cosmetic products,[6] and seekers of beauty enthusiastically agree that eggs can improve your appearance. Beaten egg whites are applied as a facial mask (egg proteins shrink as they dry, pulling at the dried layer of cells on top of your skin) to make the skin look temporarily smoother. Used in a rinse or shampoo, the protein in a beaten raw egg can make your hair look smoother and shinier by filling in chinks and notches on the hair shaft. Then again, if baldness is your problem, there is an easy solution, according to *Angry Birds: Bad Piggies' Egg Recipes*:

> Take one egg and whisk it well. Use a pastry brush to cover the bald part of the head like you would do with a pastry. Let dry for a few minutes. Don't peel it off – the head will glisten in the sun like a beautiful wet stone on a sunny beach.

Even more remarkable, in 1931 Dr Ernest Goodpasture, pathologist at Nashville's Vanderbilt University, used eggs to propagate large quantities of pure virus (uncontaminated by bacteria), the agent which produces disease. Scientists had never been able to get enough pure viruses for their experiments because unlike bacteria, viruses demand live tissue and will not multiply in artificial cultures. With associate Dr Alice Miles Woodruff, Dr Goodpasture hit on the idea of cultivating fowlpox virus in a fertile egg – a sterile medium enclosed in a naturally sterile container. After purchasing an incubator and a few dozen fertile eggs from a hatchery, Dr Goodpasture set to work. Cutting out a piece of the shell with a dentist's drill, he inoculated the thin membrane inside with infectious material, then sat back to study the results through a tiny 'window' of melted paraffin and cover glass. The fowlpox virus thrived, and subsequent tests with smallpox vaccine showed that one egg would produce enough to protect 1,000 children for life. Most of the world's HINI vaccine started in 30 chicken eggs at New York Medical College in Valhalla in 2009, thanks to Dr Goodpasture's method for developing vaccine. Although the vaccine technique might seem quaint, it continues to out-perform newer methods. 'The virus just loves to grow in the eggs,' said microbiologist Doris Butcher.[7]

Unfortunately, some children and adults suffer from severe and often life-threatening anaphylactic allergic reactions to egg whites. They are thus prevented from having standard flu vaccine shots. Ground-breaking research was begun in March 2012 by researchers at Deakin University in collaboration with the Commonwealth Scientific and Industrial Research Organisation (CSIRO), Australia's national science agency in Geelong, and the Poultry Cooperative Research Centre, which aim to produce allergy-free eggs for use in food consumption and the production of common vaccines such as flu vaccines. Of the 40 proteins in egg white there are four major allergens, and this research will systematically switch off the allergens in all four, creating a hypoallergenic egg that can produce chickens which lay allergy-free eggs. The research is expected to take three years to complete, with the possibility that allergy-free vaccines could be produced within five years, and that allergy-free eggs might be available in supermarkets for human consumption within five or ten years.

I

What Is More Perfect than an Egg?

Believe, dear friend, that no alchemist ever produced
from furnace or alembic, so rare a treasure as you may
obtain from hens, if you only know how to combine
labour and delight.

Prudent Le Choyselat, 1612

In 1751, the most ambitious publishing project of the eighteenth century was launched with the *Encyclopédie*, which aimed to encompass all knowledge of the time. Eggs were wholesome and highly nutritious, and it was believed that egg yolks were an aphrodisiac, increasing the quantity of sperm produced and promoting the sexual appetite.[1] Touted for its medicinal attributes, a poached egg with one to six drops of cinnamon oil was thought to ease prolonged labour; drunk before bedtime, egg yolk, hot water and sugar was a cure for coughs and a treatment of bilious colic; and yolks, mixed with turpentine or other natural balsams, aided digestion, certainly a questionable prescription today. Egg whites were used to prevent swelling, and to clarify pharmaceutical extracts and medicinal jellies such as the nourishing restorative Hartshorn.

'One uses it, in Medicine, for its glutinous and astringent qualities,' according to the *Encyclopédie*.

In this case one often mixes it with Armenic bole, etc., to prevent swelling in areas which suffered some violence, and to restore to the fibers their resilience and elasticity; that which one calls a preventative. It also enters in some mixes to heal recent wounds and prevent hemorrhaging.

Egg whites were also used in wine fermentation, and by book-binders and gilders to make book spines sticky before applying

Jean-Siméon Chardin, *The Attentive Nurse, c.* 1738.

gold leaf, as well as to give a lustrous shine to book covers. 'Gilders use egg white to glaire [or coat] the spine and other places two or three times with a very fine sponge, before applying the gold there once the egg white is dry,' explains the *Encyclopédie*.

> One uses the egg white again to give the covers a shine. When the book is entirely finished, one lightly wipes the entire covering with a fine sponge dipped in the egg white, and when it is dry one goes over it with the polishing iron.[2]

Leather workers also soaked the high heels of delicate ladies' shoes in egg whites before dying them with red ochre, a fashion statement at the time.

Simple in shape and elegant in appearance, an egg (in Latin, *ovum*) is pregnant with possibilities. Whether laid by a bantam, chicken, duck, gull, goose, guinea fowl, ostrich, partridge, pheasant, quail or turtle, an egg is oval (or egg shaped), usually with one end larger than the other. The one exception in birds' eggs is the perfectly round egg of an albatross – perhaps the reason why it is the only egg that is associated with bad luck. Dating back to an Indo-European root, *cheeka/e*, one who lays eggs, the derivation of the word egg comes from the Old English *oeg*. It survived in Middle English as *ey*, but in the fourteenth century the related 'egg' was borrowed from Old Norse, and has since become the common reference. 'Yolk', from the Old English word for yellow, has an Indo-European root meaning to 'gleam' or 'glitter'.[3]

'It may be the cock that crows, but it is the hen that lays the eggs,' observed Baroness Margaret Thatcher (1925–2013), Great Britain's first woman prime minister. No animal works harder than a hen to reproduce, and her effort, or fraction of

Different types of egg, a staggering variety of colour, shape and size.

body weight deposited daily in her future offspring, is 100 times greater than a human's. Each egg is about 3 per cent of her weight, so in a year of laying she converts about eight times her body weight into eggs, and a quarter of her daily energy goes towards making them. A labour of love, it takes her 24 to 26 hours to produce an egg, then she rests for 30 minutes, and begins the process all over again. She usually lays twelve eggs, called a clutch, at a time between seven and eleven in the morning, and if they are not collected, she may stop laying and start brooding.

Mrs Beeton's Book of Household Management, published in Britain in 1859, pointed out correctly that 'Eggs contain, for their volume, a greater quantity of nutriment than any other article of food.' The author's sage advice about choosing eggs was to, 'Apply the tongue to the large end of the egg, and if it feels warm, it is new, and may be relied upon as a fresh egg.'[4] Happily, it is easier today to determine whether an egg is fresh – it sinks in a bowl of water, while older eggs float. As an egg ages, air is absorbed though the shell and it loses water and carbon dioxide through the pores, making it lighter.

Biologically a reproductive unit produced by the female, an egg allows for the continuation of life, and builds a bridge between generations. After the egg cell, consisting of a ball of yolk, is fertilized, it slides down the uterine tube where the egg white (which protects the foetus and supplements the water and protein in the yolk) and shell form an egg. Each eggshell (about 12 per cent of its total weight) is composed largely of calcite, a fibre-reinforced calcium carbonate. The albumen, or white, makes up about 58 per cent, and the yolk (about 30 per cent) is anchored in place by rope-like strands of egg white called chalazae. At the rounded end of the egg is a protective pocket of air, known as the air cell or air chamber. Appearing smooth, an eggshell actually contains tiny pores (as many as 17,000) to allow moisture and carbon dioxide out and air in. When laid, an egg is warm (40°C/105°F), and as it cools the liquid contents contract, and the inner and outer shell membranes separate at the large side of the egg.

Although an egg is fragile looking, its oval shape gives it remarkable strength, and it can bear extraordinary weight on its convex surface before breaking. To determine what it takes for eggs to crack under pressure, scientists found that the average weight needed to crush a chicken egg is about $4\frac{1}{2}$ kg (10 lb), 6 kg (13 lb) for a turkey's egg, 12 kg (26 lb) for a swan's egg and 54 kg (120 lb) for a tough-shelled ostrich egg.[5] Curiously, you cannot break an egg by cupping it in the palm of your hand and squeezing because eggs are similar in shape to a three-dimensional arch, one of the strongest architectural forms. When you surround the egg with your hand, the curved form of the shell distributes pressure evenly over the shell rather than concentrating it at any one point.[6]

'The egg is a small physical thing with a beautiful geometrical surface,' wrote Martin Gardner (1914–2010), mathematics and science writer for *Scientific American*.

> It is a microcosm that obeys all the laws of the universe. And at the same time it's something far more complex and mysterious than a white pebble. It is a strange lidless box that holds the secret of life itself.

It is little wonder that the egg has been described as one of the best pieces of packaging design in the world. Amazingly, the shell is hard enough to protect the embryo in hot and dry climates, and ancient shepherds in the Middle East discovered that if they placed a raw egg in a sling and whirled it around and around, the rapid motion produced heat, cooking the egg.

It's very difficult, if not impossible, to break an egg by squeezing it like this.

These tasty packets can be kept for weeks with very little care, contain natural antimicrobial defences, making them safe for humans to eat, and are portable enough to be carried for sustenance on travels and adventures.

Occasionally – once in every 530 eggs – a hen produces double-yolk eggs during her egg-laying career, but triple-yolkers only occur once in every 5,000 eggs. It is also rare for a young hen to produce an egg with no yolk at all, something that is considered by many to be unlucky. We could not say for certain that the hen would feel the loss. In 2008, students at Yokaichi Minami High School in Japan raised a chicken that laid a large egg (8.1 cm/3¼ in and 158 g/5½ oz), which got so much attention that the school decided to put it on display. Noticing a small crack, the teachers removed the shell, and found within another perfectly formed, medium size egg. A year later the same oddity was noted by Jeff Taylor, in Ross-on-Wye, Herefordshire, in Britain; he cracked open a free-range boiled egg for his breakfast, and was shocked to find a smaller intact egg inside.

With an estimated 19 billion chickens around the globe, according to the United Nations Bahrain has the most chickens, at 40 per capita. Nearly 200 breeds and varieties exist worldwide, and the average egg-laying hen produces 270 eggs per year, almost one a day on average, weighing in at about 50 g (2 oz). Since size does matter, the largest and heaviest chicken egg in the world was laid by a Byelorussian chicken, weighing a whopping 146 g (5 oz), according to the *Guinness World Records*. In contrast, small bantam chickens lay eggs half the size of regular eggs, and chickens under a year old lay even smaller pullet eggs.

Fortunately chefs all over the world continue to ignore the riddle, 'When are cooks cruel? When they whip the eggs and beat the cream.' However, another question, 'Does anybody have a formula to calculate the boiling time for a soft-boiled egg; given its weight and initial temperature?' bothered a reader of *New Scientist* magazine. Eager to be of service, Professor C.D.H. Williams, of the University of Exeter's School of Physics, came up with the formula.[7]

Timing is everything. When eggs are cooked too long, at too high a temperature, or if the cooking water contains excessive iron, a sulphur and iron reaction can occur resulting in a greenish colour around the yolk. Scrambled eggs, too, can develop a greenish tint if they are left too long in a metal pan, although in both cases the eggs are still wholesome and flavour is unaffected. However, you do not have to brood if your cooked egg does not turn out as you wish. Physical chemist and molecular gastronomer Hervé This said you could uncook an egg with sodium borohydride, which uncoils the disulfide bridges made by heat.[8] He explains that when an egg is cooked, the protein molecules unroll themselves, link up and enclose the water molecules. To 'uncook' the egg you need to detach the protein molecules from each other. By adding sodium borohydride, the egg becomes liquid within three hours. For those who want to try this at home, vitamin C also does the trick.

Practice makes perfect for most professional cooks, who use one hand to crack an egg into a bowl. Bob Blumer, host of the American television series *Glutton for Punishment* on the Food Network, set the world record for most eggs cracked in an hour using just one hand. To best his record you would have to crack 2,071 eggs. Although he cracked 2,318 eggs, 248 were disqualified because they contained broken eggshells. When you use eggs in a recipe, break them into a separate container, so that if a shell piece falls in you can remove it.

Professor C.D.H. Williams's
Formula for Soft Boiling Eggs

The Derivation

To obtain a simple formula the problem must be idealised somewhat, so the egg will be treated as a spherical homogeneous object of mass M and initial temperature T_{egg}. If the egg is placed straight into a pan of boiling water at T_{water}, it will be ready when the temperature at the boundary of the yolk has risen to $T_{yolk} \sim 63°C$. With these assumptions, the cooking time t can be deduced by solving a heat diffusion equation.

The Result

The complete derivation is quite complicated but the final result is relatively simple:

$$t \text{ cooked} = \frac{M^{2/3} c\rho^{1/3}}{K\pi^2 (4\pi/3)^{2/3}} \log_e \left[\frac{0.76 \times (T_{egg} - T_{water})}{(T_{yolk} - T_{water})} \right]$$

where ρ is density, c the specific heat capacity, and K the thermal conductivity of 'egg'.

According to this formula, a medium egg ($M \sim 57$ g) straight from the fridge ($T_{egg}=4°C$) takes four and a half minutes to cook, but the same egg would take three and a half minutes if it had been stored at room temperature ($T_{egg}=21°C$). If all the eggs are stored in the fridge, then a small (size 6, 47 g) egg will require four minutes to cook, and a large egg (size 2, 67 g) will take five minutes.

Edible Egg Varieties

A variety of egg types apart from chicken eggs are popular food fare. Duck eggs, off-white in colour, higher in fat content and favoured in China, are oily tasting, but can be eaten in the same way as chicken eggs or used in baking. When boiled the white turns bluish, and the yolk a reddish-orange colour.

White shelled and four or five times larger than chicken eggs, goose eggs have an oily, rich taste. They are larger than light tan or ivory-coloured peacock eggs, which are about three times the size of chicken eggs. Actually, peacocks do not lay eggs; the female is a peahen. Cream coloured and specked with brown, turkey eggs are sometimes twice the size and similar in taste to chicken's eggs, so are often used as substitutes for them.[9] A speckled, iridescent ostrich egg – twenty times the size of a chicken's egg – is edible to someone with an expansive appetite, if it has not been left to bake in the sun.

On the smaller end of the size scale are guinea fowl eggs. Flecked with brown, they have a more delicate taste than a chicken's egg, and are often pickled, served hard-boiled in salads or set in aspic. Partridge eggs are white, buff or olive, although some have brown or black blotches to protect them against predators. Speckled brown quail eggs are one-third the size of a chicken's egg, and can be prepared hard-boiled, poached or in aspic. A pale rosy colour, pheasant eggs are similar in size to quails' eggs, and can be cooked in a variety of ways.

The most unique and prized eggs come from China. Salted duck egg is a Chinese preserved food product made by soaking duck eggs in brine, or packing them in damp, salted charcoal. In Asian supermarkets these eggs are often sold covered in a thick layer of salted charcoal paste, or vacuum packed without the paste. From the salt-curing process the

Twenty times the size of a chicken's egg, an ostrich egg is edible – if you have a large appetite.

duck eggs have a briny aroma, a very liquid egg white and a sharp, salty taste, and the yolk is bright orange-red in hue with a rich, fatty, but less salty taste. Normally boiled or steamed before peeling, salted duck eggs are eaten as a condiment for congee, a type of rice porridge, and cooked with other foods as a flavouring; the yolk is prized and is used in celebratory Chinese mooncakes. Marble eggs, sold by street vendors and eaten as a snack between acts at the Chinese opera, are boiled and steeped in a spicy tea mixture, which gives them a beautiful marbled appearance. Ming Dynasty eggs, fermented eggs, ancient eggs, century eggs, thousand-year-old eggs and hundred-year-old eggs are all names for the Chinese preserved duck eggs, which are covered with a coating of lime, ashes, salt and rice straw, and buried in shallow holes for up to 100 days (certainly not 1,000 years). Lime petrifies the eggs, making them look very old, and the yolks turn from amber to black with a creamy, dark green yolk. They are eaten uncooked with soy sauce and minced ginger.

Of all the edible eggs in the world, the most expensive, opulent and indulgent are fish eggs. They contain all the nutrients that one cell needs to grow into a hatchling, and are a more concentrated form of nourishment than the fish itself. A protein-rich fluid, fat-soluble carotenoid pigments, and building-block amino acids and nucleic acids surround the inner yolk of a fish egg. Roe consists of separate eggs held together in a dilute protein solution enclosed in a thin, fragile membrane.

Caviar, the salted roe of the sturgeon, is the most valued and in demand, even as civilization has encroached on its source from the landlocked Caspian Sea, which lies between Iran and Russia, putting beluga, osetra and sevruga sturgeons on the World Wildlife Foundation's Endangered Species List.

Chinese tea eggs, a great dish for Chinese New Year. The eggs symbolize golden nuggets (wealth) at a Chinese New Year feast. To get the intricate marbled effect, make sure you tap the eggs hard so that the soy sauce or tea can get through. The longer you steep the tea eggs the darker the design.

The word 'caviar' comes from the Persian *khavyar*, from *khayah*, or egg. While Western Europeans and Americans use the word caviar (it came into the English language in the sixteenth century), the Russians do not. They refer to fish roe of all kinds as *ikroj* (pronounced EEK-ruh with a rolled 'r'; the Japanese adapted the word to *ikura*). Today, white sturgeon and hackleback sturgeon are farmed in freshwater lakes or tanks in the Pacific Northwest, California and the South, using environmentally conscious and sustainable practices, making the United States a player on the world caviar scene. Other fish eggs come from bowfin, carp, cod, pollack, flying fish, grey mullet, hake, herring, lobster (eggs are referred to as coral), lumpfish, paddlefish, salmon, shad, shaker, smelt, trout, tuna and whitefish. In fact, most fish roe is edible, but that of some species, including the great barracuda and some members of the puffer (*fugu*) and trunkfish families, is toxic. Roe can be sautéed, poached or, providing it is of medium size or larger, broiled. It can also be used in sauces or to top them. The eggs of a fish are also called berries, pearls and grains. In the caviar trade, once the roe has been salted it becomes caviar.

An age-old belief in the aphrodisiac power of turtle eggs sustains a thriving black market for the forbidden ovum throughout Latin America. Most countries have banned the collection of these eggs because the world's seven sea turtle species are highly endangered by disease, fishing nets, disturbance of nesting areas and poaching of the eggs. Turtles lay their eggs in the sand on the beach, and birds and other predators, including humans, hunt for the eggs.

Alligator eggs (also the name of a shrimp-stuffed jalapeño in Cajun cooking) have a unique mild, rich flavour, making them an acquired taste. The soft shell is buff or speckled. There is another notable edible egg variety that might pique one's curiosity. When Dr Stanley Livingston tasted crocodile eggs during his Zambezi Expedition in Africa from 1858 to 1864, he remarked:

> In taste they resemble hens' eggs, with perhaps a smack of custard, and would be as highly relished by whites as blacks were it not for their unsavoury origin in man-eaters.

Arab traders in the 1300s told tales of a bird so gigantic that it could lift elephants. Sailors told them it was hunted on an island off the southern coast of Africa. Lest you think this was just a fable, archaeologists later found evidence of *Aepyornis* (the elephant bird) on Madagascar. The largest bird that ever lived, it was 3½ m (10 ft) tall and weighed about a half a ton. Its eggs were the largest ever recorded at over 8 litres (14 pints). Although *Aepyornis* could not possibly lift an elephant, the theory was never tested because no elephants lived on Madagascar. Perhaps fear of being snatched up by giant talons was the reason for the use by the Arabs of the expression 'Walking on eggshells', meaning being careful.

2

The History of Eggs

Being born in a duck yard does not matter, if only you are
hatched from a swan's egg.
Hans Christian Andersen

Our story begins with egg drawings in caves inhabited by
Cro-Magnon man, our hunter-gatherer relative who thrived
throughout Europe and the Middle East from about 230,000
to 35,000 years ago. In around 10,000 BC these hominids
curbed their wanderings, established settlements, and culti-
vated edible plants and domesticated animals to ensure a
constant supply of food no matter what the weather. Game
birds were a good source of both meat and eggs, and if eggs
were removed from the nest female jungle fowl not only laid
more eggs, but continued laying through a longer season,
increasing the egg supply.

Today's domesticated chicken and its eggs originated in
multiple places in south Asia and Southeast Asia before 7500 BC.
The chicken descends from the species *Gallus domesticus* (*gallus*
is Latin for comb). In the nineteenth century the naturalist
Charles Darwin identified the Red Jungle Fowl of Southeast
Asia as the 'progenitor of the modern barnyard chicken' and
named it *Gallus gallus*. New research confirms that the Grey

Gallus gallus, the progenitor of today's chickens.

Jungle Fowl (*G. sonneratii*) of Southern India also contributed at least one trait, its yellow skin, to the chicken's genome. Used in religious ceremonies dedicated to the Sun God in India, fowl were domesticated there by 3200 BC; chickens had scratched their way to the Tigris–Euphrates valley and Sumer before 2000 BC; and by 1500 BC pigeons and the first domesticated chickens had reached both China and Egypt.

Egyptians ate all birds' eggs, considering them wholesome when boiled, fried, poached or used to bind ingredients in sauces. As they built massive buildings, they devised a method to incubate eggs in dung heaps to increase supplies for their workers. A drawing of a pelican and a basket of eggs was found on the wall of the tomb of Haremhed, who died at Thebes in 1292 BC, so we can assume that pelican eggs provided sustenance as well. Chickens had found their way to the Polynesian islands by around 1290 BC, and to eastern Asia and Persia by 1000 BC. While the Phoenician civilization flourished from about 1200 until 332 BC, these seafarers were aficionados of ostrich eggs. Italy's first civilization, the Etruscans, who lived in ancient Italy and Corsica, raised ducks, chickens, geese, pigeons, blackbirds and partridges primarily for their eggs. Tomb paintings show men capturing the birds using nets or slings, and large numbers of eggs appear in banqueting scenes.[1]

The first written description of the egg as food is found in Mesopotamia on ancient Assyrian cuneiform tablets. It was believed that the needs of humans paralleled those of the gods, so the meals of 'gods' were served four times a day. After the 'gods' ate, the priests served the leftovers, including roasted and braised eggs, to the royal household. To commemorate his new military capital in 879 BC, the Assyrian king Assurnasirpal II hosted a ten-day banquet, attended by 69,574 of his closest friends. Offerings recorded on a stone pillar included geese, fowls, pigeons, doves, small birds and 10,000 chicken eggs.

Chickens along with their eggs flocked to Greece in around 800 BC, and arrived in Sardinia, Spain and Sicily by 600 BC. No one is certain when people started using eggs in cooking and baking, but a few ancient Greek recipes mentioning eggs date from after the time of Pericles (495–429 BC), when chickens were introduced to Africa. When hen eggs finally did enter the larder of the ancient Greeks, they were not highly regarded. *Deipnosophistai* (The Learned Banquet), a treatise on food and food preparation by Greek scholar and gourmet Athenaeus from about AD 200, ranked peacock eggs as the best of all eggs, followed by goose eggs; chicken eggs came in a distant third. Almost every Athenian owned a chicken, and they were commonly found throughout the Mediterranean, but there are very few recorded recipes with hen eggs, with the exception of *thagomata*, made from egg whites, and various stuffings using egg yolks.

The duck could be called the veteran of the hen house, since the Chinese domesticated and organized ducks in yards some 4,000 years ago, and were building egg incubators by 246 BC. In large, heated clay buildings, 36,000 eggs were turned by hand as often as five times in a 24-hour period, and hatched. A closely guarded secret, incubation methods were passed from one generation to the next, and the proper temperature was judged by placing an incubating egg in one's eye socket. Temperature changes were effected in the incubator by moving the eggs, adding additional eggs to use the heat of older eggs and regulating the flow of fresh air through the hatching area.[2]

Using eggs hatched in chambers kept warm by hot vapour in cuisine was first confirmed in Italy by the mention of eggs in a porridge recipe for *puls punica* by Roman statesman and agriculturalist Marcus Cato (234–149 BC). His recipe, which specified using a terracotta cooking pot, states:

> Add a pound of flour to water and boil it well. Pour it into a clean tub, adding three pounds of fresh cheese, half a pound of honey, and an egg. Stir well and cook in a new pot.

It is also probable that Romans ate ostrich eggs, especially if one considers that an ostrich egg is equivalent to between 24 and 28 hen eggs, making them a feast for any large gathering. Wealthy Romans took their dining seriously, and spent hours in the preparation, celebration and enjoyment of their meals. The most popular of all appetizers was the egg, and peafowl eggs were most probably their favourite eggs. They began their *coena*, or supper, with eggs as a relish, and ended it with fruit. Roman philosopher and drama critic Horace (65–8 BC) used the Latin phrase *ab ovo usque ad malum*, which literally means 'from the egg to the apples', or from the beginning of the meal to the end. As they undertook their empire-building travels, Roman soldiers found copious amounts of eggs and egg-laying hens in Britain, Scandinavia, Gaul and Germany.

During the heyday of the Roman Empire (first century BC to the late fourth century AD), *De re coquinaria* (Of Culinary Matters), the first written cookbook, debuted. Attributed to Marcus Gavius Apicius, it includes a recipe for baked custard: milk, honey and eggs beaten and cooked in an earthenware dish over a gentle heat. Apicius describes lavish feasts and exotic fare served at banquets, which often featured a drunken brawl, but if diners imbibed too much, the cure for a hangover, according to *Modern Drunkard Magazine*, was to eat fried canaries and owl eggs, fortunately not recommended today. Appetizers began with jellyfish and eggs, patina of brains cooked with milk and eggs, and sea urchins prepared with a sauce of spices, honey, olive oil and eggs. Apicius, who gluttonized on eggs with honey and pepper, calls them *ovemele*, or 'egg honey', which may be the origin of the word 'omelette'.[3] He also provided the Greek recipe for *libum*, a special cake made for religious rituals, which called for one egg to a pound of butter, offered as a sacrifice to the gods by the Romans and fed to slaves working in the temples. There is even a story of a slave boy who ran away because he could not face any more of the sweet dish. Apicius, fearing he would starve to death, reportedly poisoned himself when he realized he had no more than ten million sesterces left (equivalent to just under three-quarters of a ton of gold bullion). Different authors (ten in all) later wrote more volumes of the cookbook using the name Apicius, which came to mean 'epicure', or 'gourmet', and all but two volumes survive to this day. During the fourth century *ova spongia ex jacte*, an egg sponge with milk recipe, or pancake, made by beating four eggs with milk and oil and frying the mixture in an oiled, hot, shallow pan, appears in the Apicius series. Cooked on one side only, the sponge was served on a plate drizzled with honey and black pepper.

European cuisine was based on the belief, set forth by the Greek physician Hippocrates (460–370 BC), who proselytized 'Let your food be your medicine, your medicine be your food', a philosophy enjoying a redux today. He theorized that certain seasonings and preparation methods could eliminate imbalances and calibrate the body's bodily fluids, or four 'humours', blood, phlegm, yellow bile and black bile. Each fluid was associated with a specific personality characteristic – blood with a sanguine personality and a passionate disposition; phlegm with a personality that was sluggish and dull; yellow bile with an individual quick to anger; and black bile with a melancholic or depressed personality, *melan* meaning black. It was the

Crêpes, a classic flour and egg dish.

physician's job to restore and maintain the harmony of those four humours.

As early as the fifth century, the Roman Catholic Church prohibited parishioners from eating animal foods such as butter, cheese and eggs during Lent, the 40 days' fast preceding Easter. By the 1500s fasting had become less of an issue for Catholic households (and to some degree Lutherans and Anglicans), when the Council of Trent approved those foods.[4] With the Church's blessing, eggs became central to the daily economy, and their price was a measure of the standard of living or the value of money in any given town in any country.

Domestic fowl were bred in Ireland from at least the early Christian era, and although some believe that the Danes

Gathering eggs for cooking, from the *Tacuinum sanitatis*, 14th century.

introduced them, archaeologists tend to agree that they arrived from Roman Britain in AD 82. Most sought after were goose eggs, a luxury served at banquets on dishes of silver and gold. The residents of Blasket Island and other west-coast islanders often ate seabirds' eggs, but an unpleasant consequence of doing so was bad breath. Women and children preferred the sweeter hen eggs, whereas duck eggs were considered more substantial food for men, who took hard-boiled eggs with them for lunch when they worked in the fields. Legend also has it that the pairing of eggs and bacon is of Irish origin. As the tale goes, an old Irish peasant woman was frying bacon for her man when a hen roosting on the cross-beams above the open fireplace dropped an egg, hitting the side of the pan and spilling its contents into the sizzling fat. The woman served the dish to the man, who consumed the lot and went forth to the monastery where he laboured, marvelling at the combination. Thus the fame of bacon and eggs entered the monastery walls and spread from monastery to monastery, from country to country, as the dish came to be relished by rich and poor 'all by the grace of God and the irregular proclivities of the lazy old hen'.[5] During the Great Irish Famine (1845–7) the poor did not eat eggs; rather they were sold to pay the rent, providing up to a quarter of a poor farmer's income. Even today, when someone in Dublin is doing well financially, it is said that 'they must be keeping hens'.[6]

During the early Middle Ages (fifth to tenth century AD), feudal lords dined well on venison, beef, mutton, pork, chickens and geese – and fish on Friday – all skewered and eaten with the knives and fingers, while vassals and serfs were given eggs and cheese, along with an occasional hare or fowl. Only bread was more commonly consumed than chicken eggs, which were relatively cheap, versatile and easy to obtain by hook or by crook. Charles the Bald of France decreed in AD 844 that a bishop could requisition, at each halt in his pastoral progress, 50 loaves, ten chickens, five suckling pigs and 50 eggs, a heavy tariff if he chose to stop in a tiny hamlet.

In the middle of the Middle Ages, European nobility ate less fowl and more meat, bread and wine, although cheese and eggs were combined with meat on regular days, and alternated with fish on penitential days. Doctors of the Salerno School, who advanced a health regimen founded upon Arabic medical learning in the eleventh century (the most advanced medical knowledge of the time), recommended drinking wine to aid digestion and that eggs should always be eaten fresh and not be overcooked: *si sumas ovum, molle sit atque novum*, good advice to this day.

Anonimo, an anonymous Andalusian cookbook written in the thirteenth century, describing cookery in Spain and North Africa, records the first recipe for a food fried in egg batter, probably the origin of tempura (known to have been introduced to Japan in the sixteenth century by Portuguese Jesuits). Among the 170 recipes in the Vatican manuscript of *Le Viandier de Taillevent,* a French cookbook written in the 1300s, there are only four dishes that feature eggs as the main ingredient, although monks were known to imbibe a posset made with eggs and figs, a forerunner of eggnog.

When Buddhism became the official religion of Japan in the seventh century, Emperor Tenmu prohibited eating meat – cattle, horses, dogs, monkeys and chickens – from April through September. Oddly, the law did not apply to chicken eggs, but as ordinary people embraced Buddhism, they avoided eating eggs lest they end up in 'chicken hell', the place reserved for those who were cruel to birds. In fact, egg recipes were non-existent from the sixth to the sixteenth century in Japan. That changed in the western part of Japan from the end of the sixteenth century to the beginning of the seventeenth century due to the influence of European and Chinese traders and Christian missionaries. The first recorded egg recipe in

Eggs are an important ingredient in most cuisines.

Japan is found in *Ryori monogatari* (The Cooking Story) in 1643, with four ways to cook eggs. By 1785 there were 103 ways to cook eggs, according to *Banpo ryori himitsu bako* (How to Make a Hundred Secret Recipes), not surprising since it was believed that eggs provided increased energy, which also made them a preferred choice in brothels.[7]

Arabs in Syria, Iraq, Egypt and North Africa rarely ate eggs on their own, but chicken eggs were prized for their versatility in recipes, primarily as thickeners for sauces, as stuffings and binders, as batters and as garnishes to plates. A recipe for *makhfiya* by thirteenth-century gourmet Muhammad ibn al-Hasan ibn Muhammad ibn al-Karim al-Katib al-Baghdadi (shortened to al-Baghdadi) is a good example.

> Cut red meat into thin sliced strips . . . fry lightly . . . make into kabobs with seasonings. Take [hard] boiled egg, remove the whites, and place the yolks in the middle of the kabobs . . . Take [additional] eggs and beat well; remove the strips, dip them while still hot in the egg, and return them to the pot. Do this twice or thrice, until the slices have a coating of egg and return them to the pot.

Moorish cooks commonly beat eggs with spices and flavourings, and thickened them with flour or breadcrumbs. A recipe in the Moroccan cookbook *Fadalat al-Khiwan* calls for more eggs than any other.

> Take fatted hens and capons . . . Add water, salt, much oil, pepper, coriander, some chopped onion, peeled almonds, pine nuts, fresh acorns, fresh chestnuts and peeled blanched walnuts. Put on the fire to cook. Then take 30 eggs per bird, beat twenty of the yolks and all 30 whites [per bird] with spices.

After the birds are cooked they are combined in another pot with the beaten eggs, and served with the cooked eggs caking them, along with the reserved ten yolks, which have been fried, and then even more eggs: quartered hard-boiled eggs and a thin omelette flavoured with chicken pieces. The writer concludes: 'Eat it in good health, God the Most High Willing.'[8]

Written in the voice of a French husband addressing his young wife on proper behaviour in marriage, running a household and cooking, *Le Ménagier de Paris* (The Goodman of Paris), published in 1393, relied on egg recipes, including *oeufs perdues*, eggs broken open and poured directly onto hot embers, wiped off and eaten. Also intriguing but simple to prepare by the young bride are yolks fried in melted sugar and egg broth:

> Poach eggs in oil, then have onions sliced and cooked, and fry them in the oil, then put on to boil in wine, verjuice [an acidic, sour liquid made from unripe fruit, primarily grapes] and vinegar, and make it all boil together; then put in each bowl three or four eggs, and pour your broth over, and let it not be thick.

Many egg dishes were served in Europe by the 1400s. There was the caudel, a type of custard; jussell, made of eggs and grated bread and seasoned with saffron and sage; *froise*, a type of omelette with strips of bacon; and tansy, an omelette seasoned with chopped herbs. Cooks began glazing (or endowing) their dishes with raw egg yolk, still a popular technique in pastry making. Eggs also made their way into beverages as a prominent ingredient of wassail.[9]

There is no doubt that fine cooks experimented with eggs in every form, laying the foundations for the great period of egg cookery in French haute cuisine during the Renaissance. Eggs remained a major ingredient well into the seventeenth century, when the soufflé, cakes, mayonnaise, hollandaise and béarnaise were invented. Italian Renaissance Maestro Martino da Como, probably the first 'celebrity' chef, wrote the first known culinary guide to specify ingredients, cooking times, techniques and utensils, in around 1450. *The Art of Cooking* includes his best-known recipe for *frictata,* or frittata, made with eggs beaten with a little water and milk, grated cheese, parsley, borage, mint, marjoram, sage or other herbs. He not only devoted an entire chapter to eggs, but invented *raffioli,* a progenitor of ravioli, by wrapping eggs in pasta dough. Most intriguing is his exotic recipe for frying an egg, then removing the yolk, mixing it with grated cheese, mint, parsley and raisins, and replacing this mixture in the hole. He then refries the egg and tops it with orange juice and ginger.

Scholars of the Iberian Peninsula have gleaned what common people ate as well by examining the account books of hospitals and monasteries. At the monastery of San Pedro in Toledo, Spain, the account books for 1455–8 and 1485–98 indicate that the diets of the poor were lean. They ate boiled, tough meat, while the friars enjoyed veal and partridges, and chickens stuffed with eggs, saffron, cinnamon and sugar.[10] Meanwhile the Janissaries, the elite corps of Christian youths recruited by Ottoman Turkish sultans and converted to Islam, were highly respected for their military prowess in the fifteenth and sixteenth centuries. Better fed than the general population, they loved a pudding made from wine and eggs mixed with plenty of sugar and spices.[11] Greeks are famous for their chicken rice soup with an *avgolemomo,* or egg lemon sauce, made with raw egg yolks beaten into a hot meat or poultry broth with added lemon, which is also poured over meat balls, stuffed vegetables and stuffed vine leaves. But this egg emulsion has a long history. In 1453, the Turkish Ottomans conquered Constantinople, which resulted in a feud that continues to this day between the Turks and the Greeks. During the celebratory festivities, the conqueror Mehmet II was served *terbiyali* sauce, almost the identical recipe of eggs beaten into broth the Greeks claim to have invented.

One of the earliest culinary historians, Bartolomeo Sacchi, writing as Platina, compiled the first printed Italian cookbook in the summer of 1465, and it was a monument to medieval cuisine compiled during the Renaissance. *De honesta voluptate et valetudine* (On Honourable Pleasure and Health) included a recipe for roasted eggs:

> Turn fresh eggs carefully in warm ashes near the fire so that they cook on all sides; When they begin to leak they are thought to be freshly done, and so are served to guests. These are the best and are most agreeably served.

Egg recipes proliferated in sixteenth-century Europe. Because of a sudden spike in the population, coupled with rampant inflation, the average family was forced to find alternatives to expensive meat. Egg farming became increasingly profitable as the Italian Renaissance spread north. Replacing breadcrumbs as a thickener, eggs became binders in most recipes, and egg yolks were used as flavour enhancers. Cooks experimented with new ways to cook eggs – from barely cooked *ova sorbilia* – to poached, fried, baked, roasted and even grilled eggs, along with omelettes, custards, zabaglione and garnishes.

When Catherine de Medici married France's King Henry in 1533, she introduced spinach into Gallic cuisine. In honour of her birthplace, Florence, the French coined the phrase *à la Florentine* for dishes prepared with spinach and topped with a mornay cheese sauce. Those early recipes for eggs Florentine paired ingredients with poached or baked eggs.

Fried eggs.

Later some recipes called for hard-boiling the eggs, others for scrambling. Over the years, chefs have taken liberties with eggs Florentine. In his 1898 cookbook *Eggs and How to Use Them*, Adolphe Meyer, chef at Manhattan's exclusive Union Club, describes them as 'eggs dressed in a chicken and mushroom cream sauce poured over not spinach but the bottoms of artichokes', ironically another vegetable introduced to France by the same queen.

By the 1540s cookbooks had appeared in France, Britain and Italy; it was the true beginning of ovophilia. The *Livre fort excellent de Cuysine* (The Most Excellent Book of Cookery) offers many egg recipes, but the *pièce de résistance* is eggs boiled in water and coloured. The dye extract *Rubia tinctorum* was used for red eggs. Onion peel gave eggs a yellow hue, and gold leaf apparently made them violet, although it is unclear how that occurred. Even more intriguing is a recipe for eggs cooked without fire. Eggs were nestled in a basket of lime (calcium carbonate), then dipped in water. In another cookbook, *Proper Newe Book of Cokerye*, written at about the same time, eggs are used in custards and fritters, and in tarts in both the pastry and filling. However, the most famous recipe was 'egges in moneshyne', egg yolks poached in melted sugar and rosewater – intended to resemble a bright moon in a limpid sky.[12] During this period one is hard pressed to find a recipe that does not use eggs. In the Italian cookbook *Libro Novo* (New Book) by Christoforo Messisbugo, egg yolks were incorporated into his Hungarian egg soup, which calls for 40 eggs, verjuice, butter and sugar lightly cooked in a bain marie (water bath) until thickened. An obsession with eggs is also apparent in Bartolomeo Scappi's *Opera* (1570), which contains a recipe for *uova da bere*, or drinkable eggs. Fresh eggs are pierced with a pin and boiled for a *credo* (about 30 seconds) until the eggs will spin, or are too hot to hold in the hand. The top is broken off, and the contents are sprinkled with salt and sugar and drunk directly from the shell.

Francisco Martínez Motiño, master chef to Philip III of Spain, published *Arte de cocina, pasteleria, bizcocheria y conserveria* in 1611 – important for the fact that he was the first to discuss kitchen organization. His advice for the cook was to pay attention to three things: cleanliness, taste and speed. His Christmas banquet incorporates eggs in little veal puff-pastry pies, bird tartlettes over whipped cream soup, hollow cakes, *capirotada* (batter of herbs and eggs), leavened puff pastry with pork lard, thin hard-baked cake with quince sauce, quince pastries, eggs beaten with sugar, hare *empanadas* and puff-pastry tart. By the middle of the 1600s, leading French gastronomes began advocating for harmony in cooking based on flavour for its own sake, and that led to the development of butter and cream sauces. Paris kitchens were the research and development laboratories of classic French sauces thickened by emulsification, which achieve their texture through the suspension of tiny droplets of one liquid in another with which it cannot freely mix. Emulsifying agents – including some of the proteins, salts and fatty acids in milk solids and egg yolks – stabilize suspension of the droplets by bonding with water and oil molecules, creating a slightly viscous texture, which is why beating an egg into vinaigrette turns it into a single creamy mass.

Lavish cuisine and glutinous portions held sway in French kitchens until the seventeenth century, when a population

Diego Velázquez, *Old Woman Cooking Eggs*, 1618.

boom led to suburban expansion. Seeking bucolic escapes, rich Parisians purchased farms and vineyards. A profusion of newly available garden-fresh ingredients in turn inspired techniques that enhanced the foods' intrinsic qualities. Called *le goût naturel* (the natural taste) by valet to Louis XIV Nicolas de Bonnefons, vegetables took centre place on the plate, served with delicate, sauces, including one cream sauce thickened with egg yolks, described in Bonnefons' 1651 cookbook *Le Jardinière français* (The French Garden).

Modern hollandaise sauce, béarnaise sauce and other sauces are descendants of one of the greatest chefs of that time, François Pierre de La Varenne (1618–1678). He wrote *Le Cuisinier françois* (The French Cook), one of the most influential cookbooks of all time and the first with recipes in alphabetical order. He frowned on spices, and provided 60 recipes for the formerly humble egg, treated vegetables as food in their own right, and created sauces based on meat drippings, combined merely with vinegar, lemon juice, or verjuice. Published in 1653, the cookbook introduced the recipe 'Eggs in the Moon Shine with Cream', or fried eggs. La Varenne's *la sauce blanche* (white sauce), a combination of egg yolks with acidic liquid and butter, achieves its denser but silky texture from the emulsifying power of egg yolks. Due to the presence of phospholipids, a single large egg yolk can bind up to 110 g (4 oz) of butter in a sauce, and higher amounts of oil in cold sauces such as mayonnaise. A differentiation was made between ragouts, which tended to use a flour and butter roux, and fricassees, which used egg yolks in *Le Cuisinier royal et bourgeois* (The Court and Country Cook), by François Massialot (1660–1733), who cooked at Versailles. The absence of graininess was a novel change from the classic medieval sauces, which relied on combinations of breadcrumbs, pounded almonds or croutons simmered in bouillon.

The fats in the egg yolks and roux – not to mention the cream and additional butter used as enrichments – also produced a certain mouth-filling voluptuousness.

Massialot's cookbook includes the first printed recipe for crème brûlée, a sweet dessert custard of egg yolks and milk with a burned crust of sugar, although a similar recipe for *crema catalana*, custard topped with crystallized sugar, dates back to medieval times in Spain. It was the Spanish dessert that inspired Sirio Maccioni, owner of Le Cirque, to ask his pastry chef Dieter Schorner to develop a spin-off for his menu in the 1980s, which kicked off the current global trend. It was cooked in a shallow, fluted casserole, the shell was thinner and the name was gallicized to crème brûlée to fit in at the French restaurant in New York.[13]

Princess Palatine, sister-in-law of Louis XIV, wrote of his incredible appetite in 1718:

> He could eat four plates of soup, a whole pheasant, a partridge, a large plate of soup, a whole pheasant, a partridge, a large plate of salad, two slices of ham, mutton au jus with garlic, a plate of pastry, all followed by fruit and hard-boiled eggs.

A love of eggs ran in the family. Louis XV (1715–1774) ate oiled eggs every Sunday, and Parisians admired their sovereign's dexterity with an egg. In an almost religious hush, he would knock the small end off the egg with a single stroke of his fork, while an officer of the table called for attention, announcing, 'The King is about to eat his egg!'

It was not only royalty who craved eggs. After failing to make an omelette, Napoleon Bonaparte (1769–1821) is purported to have exclaimed: 'I have given myself credit for more exalted talents than I possess.' This was quite an admission

Sèvres egg cup,
1756–68.

from the general, who believed that 'an army marches on its stomach', was a wine aficionado and encouraged canning as a way to safely preserve food.

After the French Revolution (1789–1814), fancy food and entertaining were all the rage again, led by diplomat Charles-Maurice de Talleyrand-Périgord. From 1797 he employed a cook and former baker named Antonin Carême, who turned out to be one of the greatest culinary geniuses of the nineteenth century. He knew the foibles and the favourite dishes of the Romanovs, Rothschilds and Rossini. He even made Napoleon's wedding cake.[14] Carême, who loved complex shapes and decorations, devised a recipe for 'Eggs Carême': eggs baked in cylindrical moulds until the whites were set, with a garnish of truffles and pickled ox tongue. Each unmoulded egg was then nestled in a poached artichoke bottom; layered with a ragout of lambs' sweetbreads, truffles and mushrooms; topped with a brown sauce flavoured with Madeira wine and cream; and finally garnished with a slice of tongue cut into a saw-tooth pattern. Most importantly, Carême, the first chef to become rich and famous by publishing cookbooks, developed a methodology by which hundreds of sauces could be categorized under five principal sauces: hollandaise sauce (butter), tomato sauce (red), bechamel sauce (white), velouté sauce (blond) and brown or espagnole sauce (demi-glace). Of the principal sauces only hollandaise contains eggs, but today they are used in many popular sauce variations – aioli, garlic-flavoured mayonnaise made from pounded cloves of garlic, egg yolks, oil and seasoning, with lemon juice and a little cold water added before serving; béarnaise, a variation of hollandaise made with egg yolks, white wine or vinegar, diced shallots, tarragon and peppercorns; newburg, composed of butter, cream, egg yolks, sherry and seasonings; and remoulade, a chilled flavoured sauce of mayonnaise, anchovies or anchovy paste, mustard, capers and chopped pickles, a New Orleans favourite.

Pavlova, a meringue with cream and berries.

Often called the greatest chef of all time, chef of kings and king of chefs, French master chef Georges Auguste Escoffier (1846–1935) cooked his way into culinary history. He co-created the Ritz Hotel chain, became known as the ambassador of French cuisine, inspired chefs all over the world and was eventually knighted for his many contributions. Escoffier was so slight that he wore platform shoes to enable him to reach the stove. His size did not prevent him from reaching the heights of culinary expertise by refining and simplifying grande cuisine and making preparation more efficient. His *Le Guide culinaire* (1902) listed more than 300 egg dishes, and has become the most definitive cooking reference for chefs to this day. His scrambled eggs were world famous. Kaiser Wilhelm ii once remarked to Escoffier: 'I am the emperor of Germany, but you are the emperor of chefs.'

3
No Eggs, No Cuisine

A hard-boiled egg is hard to beat.

Anonymous

Eggs are an important ingredient in almost all cuisines, they are a key ingredient in lacto-ovo vegetarian meals. They can take centre stage in omelettes, quiches, frittatas and other entrées; sometimes they are supporting players used for their functionality in recipes for baked foods such as cakes, pastries and brownies. One of nature's most perfect foods, an egg yolk and an egg white magnificently balance each another, and individually they are unique. When the yolk – whose fat destroys the albumen's ability to foam – is removed from the white and used separately, it binds ingredients, adds a creamy, smooth texture to baked goods, sauces, puddings and custards, provides a rich colour and flavour, and emulsifies sauces. Egg whites provide strength, stability and moisture to baked goods. When whipped, egg-white proteins break and expand, and form elastic walled cells that trap air, which expand when subjected to heat, making them a valuable leavening agent. They are used to lighten the texture and increase the volume of baked goods. Egg-white foams appear to be potential structure builders in sour dough and may serve as alternative structural agents in increasingly popular gluten-free baked foods. Meringues and dessert mousses obtain smooth and fluffy consistencies due to eggs; fried foods are often cooked with an egg and flour coating; and beaten eggs, when added to a hot soup, garnish the dish.

It is important to remember that eggs should be at room temperature if they are to be combined with a fat and a sugar. Cold eggs may harden the fat in a recipe, causing the batter to curdle and affecting the texture of the finished dish. If you keep eggs in the refrigerator, remove them an hour or so before baking, or put them in a bowl of warm water for a few minutes while assembling other ingredients.

Nutritionally, one hen egg contains thirteen nutrients and 6 g of protein. All of the fat, three-quarters of the calories and a little less than half of the protein reside in the yolk, which also contains vitamins A, D and E and zinc, and carotenoids, which give yolks their colour. The colour can be enhanced by adding natural yellow-orange marigold petals to a hen's diet. The yolk has more phosphorus, thiamine, manganese, iron, iodine, copper and calcium than the white, which boasts more riboflavin and niacin. In a large egg all of that nutrition is packed into about 70 calories, and eggs are rated 1.0, or a perfect score, on the Protein Digestibility Corrected Amino Acid Score (PDCAAS). Nature's great emulsifier, the yolk produces a stable mixture of food components – oils, fats, water, air, carbohydrates, proteins, minerals, vitamins and flavours – blending the ingredients and preventing them from separating during cooking and processing.

Hen eggs are usually either white or brown in colour, although there are some rare breeds that lay blue or green eggs. As a general rule, breeds with white feathers and ear lobes lay white eggs; those with red feathers and ear lobes lay brown eggs. White eggs are most in demand among American buyers, but they have the same nutritional value as brown eggs. The latter do have harder shells, which make them ideal for hard-boiling. You can tell if an egg is hard-boiled by placing it on its side and spinning it. If the egg wobbles and stops spinning, it is not cooked; if it spins freely, it is hard-boiled. And in case you wondered, a shelled egg cannot be cooked in a microwave oven.

A $7 billion-dollar industry, some 78 billion (or 6.5 billion dozen) eggs, or 10 per cent of all the world's supply of hen eggs, are produced in the United States each year. Of this amount, 60 per cent is used by consumers, who eat an average of 249 eggs per year, 9 per cent is used by the food-service industry, and the rest is turned into egg products

'Fight food waste in the home', u.s. advertising campaign advising on food preserva-tion, c. 1945.

for restaurants and incorporated into prepared retail foods by manufacturers.

Seeking to come up with new uses for eggs, the food industry today continues to develop processed and convenient forms of eggs for commercial, food-service and home sales. Refrigerated liquid, frozen, dried and speciality products compare in flavour, nutritional value and usage with shell eggs. Convenience foods like cake and pudding mixes, pasta, ice cream, mayonnaise, sweets and bakery goods all use egg products as an ingredient. Preferred to shell eggs by commercial bakers, food manufacturers and the food-service industry, these egg products are more convenient to use, portion controlled, save labour, have minimal storage requirements and provide higher product quality, stability and uniformity.

Surplus shell eggs are also used in making egg products, and 'blown-out' shell eggs can be used in any cooked recipe that calls for mixed yolks and whites. By 1992 about 20 per cent of total u.s. egg production went into egg products; today about three-quarters of a billion pounds of all types of egg product are produced each year. To make refrigerated liquid products, eggs are broken and separated by machines and the liquid egg is put into covered containers, then shipped to bakeries for immediate use or to plants for further processing. Shipment in sanitary tank trucks maintains temperatures low enough to ensure that the liquid egg arrives at its destination at 4°C (40°F) or less. Frozen egg products include separated whites and yolks, whole eggs, blends of whole eggs and yolks, and whole eggs and milk. Salt or carbohydrates are sometimes added to yolks and whole eggs to prevent gelation during freezing. Produced in the u.s. since 1930, dried or dehydrated egg products are known as egg solids. Demand was minimal until the Second World War, when production reached peak levels to meet increased requirements for feeding the military stationed abroad. Dried egg products today are used in many convenience foods and in the food-service industry.

Egg specialities for the food-service industry include wet-pack and dry-pack, pre-peeled, hard-cooked eggs, either whole, wedged, sliced, chopped or pickled; long rolls of hard-cooked eggs; frozen omelettes; egg patties; quiche and quiche mixes; frozen French toast; frozen scrambled egg mixes in boilable pouches; frozen fried eggs; frozen pre-cooked scrambled eggs; freeze-dried scrambled eggs, and other convenience menu items. Quail eggs, as hard-cooked, shelf-stable, packaged products, are now featured on many gourmet food counters in the U.S. and Japan. Innovative egg products – ultra-pasteurized liquid egg, free-flowing frozen egg pellets and modified atmosphere packaging for hard-cooked eggs – will soon be readily available. Many speciality egg items are reaching the retail market as well, including frozen omelettes and mixes; frozen scrambled eggs, French toast and quiche; and specially coated, shelf-stable, hard-cooked eggs.

Naturally nutrient-dense eggs are in demand all over the world. Key major global processors of hen eggs include Cal-Maine Foods Inc., Hy-Line International, Keggfarms Pvt. Ltd, Land O'Lakes Inc., Michael Foods Inc., Ningbo Jiangbei Dexi Foods Co. Ltd, Nobel Foods Ltd, Rose Acre Farms Inc., Pilgrim's Pride Corporation, Suguna Poultry Farm Limited, Tree of Life Inc. and Tyson Foods.[1] The global market for eggs is expected to reach 1,154 billion by the year 2015, and the Asian Pacific, especially China, which produces 390 billion chicken eggs per year, is expected to account for half the world's supply. China also produced 5.5 million tons of duck eggs, making it the world's largest supplier. After centuries of practice to perfect duck dishes, they remain the pride of Chinese cuisine. Annual consumption is also highest in China, at 333 eggs per person. Most egg production is done in large-scale integrated operations. Chinese producers now typically confine egg-laying hens in small wire 'battery' cages stacked in rows in sheds that are the length of a football field, but the cage-free movement is growing there. Eggs are a vital component of the average Chinese diet, and cooks often use lacy ribbons of cooked egg, or egg shreds, as garnishes, and they are incorporated into soups and tofu paste, and used as additives and ingredients.

India, where egg is used as a binder and in various curry dishes, is the second largest egg producer, but consumption is low, at 48 eggs per person, in this primarily vegetarian nation. With a population of 1.2 billion and a government plan encouraging egg-protein consumption, India is one of the fastest growing markets, according to the International Egg Commission (IEC).

Japan is third in production, and per capita egg consumption is 320. It is the single largest importer of U.S. egg products. Eggs in Japan are eaten on, with and in almost everything, and twenty eggs can be bought for the price of a single bowl of noodles. Japanese consumers prefer raw eggs; a raw egg and soy sauce on rice constitutes a simple, quick meal. An egg broken into a bowl of hot rice, stirred and eaten lightly scrambled is the most popular breakfast choice. Served communally, *sukiyaki* and *shabu-shabu* include a whisked egg dipping sauce on the side. Almost any meat or poultry coated with bread-like *panko* crumbs and fried becomes the centrepiece of a frittata-like egg dish served over rice. One of the most popular sushi dishes, Tamago Roll, the Japanese name for a sweet egg om-elette, comprises layers of egg rolled back and forth across one another in a special rectangular pan designed just for that use.

Today, the majority of eggs consumed in Mexico (300 eggs per capita), the fourth largest producer of eggs, are chicken eggs, with quail eggs a distant second. Eggs were introduced

Migas, a traditional Tex-Mex breakfast.

to the Aztecs by Spanish conquistadors in the 1500s. They are an integral part of the national culinary repertoire, although recipes are regionally different, and indispensable in flan, *huevos reales*, *cocada* and other desserts, and a wide array of savoury egg preparations, such as *huevos rancheros*, *huevos al albañil* (brick-layers' eggs) topped with green chilli and tomatillo sauce, and *huevos divorciados* (divorced eggs), so named because the dish consists of two eggs, each in a different sauce, one red and one green. Eggs scrambled with leftover tortillas constitute an economical meal that gave rise to the Tex-Mex dish called *migas*, literally meaning 'crumbs', possibly a descendant of the Spanish dish of the same name, which combines cubes of leftover country bread with eggs.[2]

Thailand's stuffed eggs, *kai kwam*, are filled with a mix-ture of seafood and pork, then seasoned with fish sauce, coconut milk and cilantro. The egg halves are filled, dipped in batter and deep fried until golden. While Australians enjoy the classic devilled egg, they have the most unique variation:

Pickled eggs are often found on the shelves of British fish and chip shops, or sometimes behind the counter of selected pubs. These ones have been pickled with beetroot.

the devilled greenish emu egg. Creator Paul Tessmer suggests boiling the grapefruit-sized egg for 70 minutes. Since the shell supports the weight of a 68 kg (150 lb) bird, cracking it requires the use of a crab mallet or heavy kitchen knife. The large egg white is cut into 2½ cm (1 in) squares and filled with yolk, mayonnaise, ketchup, Worcestershire sauce and relish.

Consumers in Austria, Denmark, France, Germany, Italy, Hungary and New Zealand eat more than 200 eggs per capita each year. Over the past four decades there has been a ten-fold increase in egg consumption in developing countries with growing populations and rising incomes, including Libya,

Colombia, where whole eggs are one of many fillings for cornflour fritters called *arepas*, and Turkey, where a staple of Turkish cuisine is *menemem*, a scrambled egg and vegetable dish. Turkish chefs set a new world record for the world's largest omelette in October 2010, when they cooked the dish in a 10 m (1,345 ft) round frying pan using 110,000 eggs.

Originally created at the Changa Restaurant in Istanbul by chef Peter Gordon, but also served at his Providores Restaurant in London, Turkish Eggs is a unique dish. Two perfectly poached eggs sit on a pillow of whipped yoghurt wrapped in hot chilli butter; they provide an unforgettable taste experience. Also distinctive and unusual, though a little more commonplace in Britain, are pickled eggs, often pickled with beets for colour. Curiously reminiscent of medical specimens because they are bottled, they are often found on the shelves of British fish and chip shops, and sometimes behind counters at selected pubs. If you are tempted to pickle your own, a curious website called Egg Pub offers a basic recipe.

Torhonya, or *rivilhus* as they are sometimes called, are tiny chewy dumplings made of egg and flour, and added to soups in Austria, Hungary and other Central European countries. Made fresh and cooked in the pot after the meat and vegetables have been cooked, they require slow cooking, much like other peasant dishes that stick to the ribs. Although quiche is considered a classic dish of French cuisine, it actually originated in Germany, in the medieval kingdom of Lothringen when it was under German rule; the French later renamed it Lorraine. The word 'quiche' is from the German '*kuchen*', meaning cake. The original 'quiche Lorraine' was an open pie filled with an egg and cream custard with smoked bacon. Cheese was later added and the bottom crust, originally made from bread dough, evolved into a shortcrust or puff-pastry crust. Quiche became popular in Britain sometime after the Second

Quiche Lorraine, a classic egg, cheese and bacon dish.

World War, and in the u.s. during the 1950s. Because of its primarily vegetarian ingredients, it was considered a somehow 'unmanly' dish, as in 'real men don't eat quiche'.

In Spain a tortilla is a type of omelette, most commonly covered with potatoes and eaten at any meal. Along with paella and gazpacho, the Spanish tortilla is an icon of Iberian cooking. Called *tortilla de patatas*, or *tortilla espanola*, it is ubiquitous in bars, restaurants and homes, and is consumed for breakfast, lunch and dinner, and as a snack and a late-night nibble. So quickly are tortillas devoured that they are often left out, unrefrigerated, on the dining room table, in the way French families store cheese in a cupboard. No self-respecting tapas bar is without tortillas. The humble egg and potato dish is sliced into cubes, skewered with toothpicks and set out on long, wooden, stand-up bars in all regions of the country.

Italian dessert making incorporates dishes that provide pleasure above all else, so desserts are notable lavish arrangements of indulgent ingredients and truly unforgettable flavour combinations. The most popular fare is undoubtedly tiramisu, an elegant velvety, rich dessert made by combing ladyfinger biscuits, espresso, mascarpone cheese, eggs, sugar, Marsala wine, rum and cocoa powder. The name 'tiramisu' translates into 'pick-me-up', and there are two divergent accounts as to why the dish has this name. The first suggests that the name means 'a pick me up', referring to the two caffeinated ingredients – espresso and cocoa – present in the dish. The second refers to the idea that the dish is so wonderful that it makes the taster swoon, warranting the person who is eating it to state the request 'pick me up'. Le Beccherie Restaurant in Treviso, Italy, is most often credited with having invented this heavenly dessert in 1971. However, some say it was developed during the First World War for men to take with them when sent off to war, being offered in the hope that it would give the soldiers more energy and ensure their safe return. A third potential source of origin affirms that the tiramisu has a much lengthier lineage, since there were recipes for similar layered deserts in Tuscany during the seventeenth century.

Tiramisu, a delicious dish of mascarpone, eggs, ladyfingers and coffee.

Balut, a developing duck embryo, eaten boiled in its shell.

Zabaglione, or *zabaione*, is another popular Italian dessert, consisting of egg yolks, sugar and wine (typically Marsala) whisked together over heat until the mixture froths; it is generally served in glasses. *Zabaglion*, a variation of the dessert created in Venice, is very popular in Venezuela. There the main ingredients are egg yolks, sugar, cream, mascarpone and occasionally sweet wine. Traditionally it is served with fresh figs.

Spaghetti alla carbonara, a combination of pasta, cured pork, eggs and cheese, is one of the most popular dishes in the world. It is believed that this creation dates back only to the last years of the Second World War, when there were many servicemen in Rome after the city was liberated from the Germans in 1944. Roman cooks invented the recipe to make use of the American supplies of bacon and powdered eggs, and combined the ingredients with the pasta loved by the Italians. Food historians agree that it is a variant of a dish long enjoyed in central and southern Italy, namely *pasta cacio e uova*, pasta dressed with melted lard, and mixed with beaten eggs and grated cheese, a recipe that appeared in *La Cucina teorico pratica* (The Theoretical and Practical Kitchen), a book edited in 1837 by Neapolitan Ippolito Cavalcanti, Duke of Buonvicino.

Called *būrak* in Algeria and *brīwat* in Morocco, Tunisia's *brīk* (pronounced 'breek') is a deep-fried, crispy, brown savoury pastry, with a runny egg yolk and white, eaten with the fingers and popular as a street food. Turkish cookbook writer Ayla Esen Algar mentions one account that attributes the invention of *börek* to Bugra Khan (*d*. 994), a ruler of eastern Turkistan, from where it gradually spread westwards to Khorasan and finally to the Mediterranean.

Filipinos prefer *balut*, or fertilized duck eggs. Depending on the age of the egg, an embryo can include a beak, bones and feathers. Men eat *balut* for its alleged aphrodisiac properties, while women eat it for energy and nutrition; as the national street food of the Philippines, it is often described as being as 'popular in Manila as hot dogs are in the United States'. *Balut* is also a popular snack for Chinese, Laotians, Cambodians, Hawaiians and Thais, and is popular in California, with its large population of Filipino-Americans. Arriving in the Philippines in the 1500s, Spaniards also brought their taste for sweets with the introduction of *leche* flan (milk custard), or crème brûlée, *yema* (egg yolk sweets), *torta del rey* (the king's cake) and *hojaldres*, *rosquillos, enseimada* and *galletas* (biscuits). Thus eggs provide endless creative opportunities for professional and amateur chefs alike in sweet and savoury dishes, as a result of their convenience of use and adaptability.

4
Eggs in American Cuisine

I'm youth, I'm joy, I'm a little bird that has broken out of the egg.
James M. Barrie

Some believe that Christopher Columbus brought the first chickens to the New World on his second voyage in 1493. The first English colonists carried chickens to Virginia on the *Mayflower* in 1620, but the unacclimatized hens disappointed their owners by not laying at first. Later colonists brought their favourite cookery books and adapted ingredients and cooking techniques. Published in England in 1615, *The English Huswife* by Gervase Markham contained a popular white pudding recipe incorporating sweet cream, oatmeal steeped in milk for twelve hours, eight egg yolks, beef suet and spices – ingredients that were readily available.

A small, brown, leather-bound volume written by Frances Parke Custis, divided into *A Booke of Cookery*, with 205 recipes, and *A Booke of Sweetmeats*, with 326 recipes, is a treasure available in the Division of Manuscripts of the Historical Society of Pennsylvania. It was brought to Mount Vernon early in the summer of 1759 by Colonel George Washington's new 27-year-old wife Martha, whose first husband had been Mrs Custis's son. Eggs were customarily served on large platters,

William Hogarth, *Columbus Breaking the Egg*, 1752. Legend has it that after Christopher Columbus discovered America, others played down the accomplishment. Columbus challenged some to balance an egg on its end – and none could. He then slightly cracked the egg on the table and balanced it. His point was that everything looks easy once you see how it is done.

'sunny side up', with ribbons of crisp bacon for breakfast, but eggs were largely ignored in the cookbook, other than as ingredients. However, a speciality recipe, Buttered Eggs, was duly set down. Although the quantities of ingredients seem enormous, it was not unusual for a family to have ten or twelve children along with other relatives at the table. A Black Cake recipe calls for 'twenty eggs, two pounds of butter, two pounds of sugar, and a quart of cream'.[1]

Working as a domestic in colonial America, Amelia Simmons published *American Cookery* at her own expense in Hartford, Connecticut, in 1796. It was the first American cookbook to adapt traditional dishes by using Native

American ingredients such as cornmeal and squash, which were included in Indian Slapjack, Johnny Cake and Squash Pudding. Her advice was to always use fresh eggs. In 1897, Florence Eckhardt of the Ladies' Aid society explained how to check them:

> Eggs – Clear, thin shell'd, longest oval and sharp ends are best; to ascertain whether new or stale – hold to the light, if the white is clear, the yolk regularly in the centre, they are good – but if otherwise, they are stale. The best possible method of ascertaining, is to put them into water, if they lye on their bilge, they are good and fresh – if they bob up on end they are stale, and if they rise they are addled, proved, and of no use.[2]

Not everyone raised chickens, so in the mid-1800s market day became increasingly important. The centre of a town was the public square, where business was transacted, merchandise was bartered, and families who lived great distances from each other discussed politics and socialized. Since the majority of settlers worked long hours, Saturday was designated as the day to take the wagon or horse to town to stock up on supplies. 'Saturday was a great day, when from many miles around the old and young, male and female, came with every product of the land, by every means of conveyance, to trade,' wrote William Henry Milburn, a Methodist Episcopal clergyman and author of *Ten Years of Preacher Life*, who lived in Jacksonville, Illinois.

> Homespun dames and damsels, making the circuit of the square inquiring at every door: 'D'ye buy eggs and better yer?' and sometimes responding indignantly, as I heard a maiden when told that eggs were bringing only three cents

a dozen: 'What, do ye s'pose our hens are gwine to strain theirselves a laying eggs at three cents a dozen? Lay 'em youself, and see how you'd like the price.

Descended from posset, a British hot drink made of eggs and milk, and combined with ale, wine or cider, eggnog, which was and still is used in toasts to prosperity and good health, was first recorded in 1825. Also called an egg flip, nog referred to a strong type of beer brewed in East Anglia in England. Mark Morton, author of *Cupboard Love: A Dictionary of Culinary Curiosities* (1997), suggests that the term 'nog' may be related to 'noggin', a word for a cup that held only a quarter of a pint of ale or other drinking liquid. He goes on to say that it is probably related to noggin, 'head', the skull being a kind of cup for the brain. Affluent gentlemen in Britain mixed sugar, milk and eggs with brandy, Madeira or sherry. In fact, an early British slang term for a potent hot beer, egg and brandy libation was Huckle My Buff, according to the *Dictionary of the Vulgar Tongue* (1811). Eggnog became even more popular in America, where dairy products were plentiful and Caribbean rum was inexpensive. George Washington even penned his own famous, heavy-on-the-alcohol eggnog recipe, but forgot to record the exact number of eggs he used (cooks estimate a dozen would do).

One quart cream, one quart milk, one dozen tablespoons sugar, one pint brandy, ½ pint rye whiskey, ½ pint Jamaica rum, ¼ pint sherry – mix liquor first, then separate yolks and whites of eggs, add sugar to beaten yolks, mix well. Add milk and cream, slowly beating. Beat whites of eggs until stiff and fold slowly into mixture. Let set in cool place for several days. Taste frequently.

Variations of eggnog are found in many countries, albeit by different names. In Puerto Rico *coquito* is made with eggs, and fresh coconut juice or coconut milk mixed with rum. In Mexico *rompope* is augmented with cinnamon and rum or grain alcohol, and sipped as a liqueur. In Peru *biblia con pisco* is made with Peruvian pomace brandy called *pisco* and is popular during holiday celebrations. The Dutch serve *advocaat* (from *advocatenborrel*), a liqueur made with brandy, sugar and eggs. Of Vietnamese origin, *soda sữa hột gà*, also known as egg soda, is a sweet drink made from egg yolk, sweetened condensed milk and club soda. It is also consumed in Cambodia. *Kogel mogel* (*gogel mogel* in Yiddish), made from egg yolks, sugar and flavourings such as chocolate or rum, is popular in Poland and qualifies more as a dessert than a drink. As already mentioned in chapter Three, zabaglione, also known as *zabayon* and *saboyon*, is a simple Italian custard dessert made with egg yolks, sugar and Marsala wine. *Eierpunsch* (literally 'egg punch') is the German name given to a warm drink made with egg whites, sugar, white wine and vanilla; it is served in the popular Christmas markets of Germany and Austria. One of the traditional drinks of Venezuela, and prepared to celebrate the festival of Navideñas, *ponche crema* is basically made of milk, sugar, rum, spices and eggs. It is notable that the recipe varies from one region of the country to another. *Tamagozake* (translated as 'egg sake') is a drink consisting of heated sake, sugar and a raw egg that is served in Japan. A word to the wise – eggnog can contain upwards of 400 calories per cup. Whatever version you prefer, eggnog is celebrated on 24 December, Eggnog Day.[3]

Lydia Maria Child, a writer of romantic novels and books for children, and editor of abolitionist newspapers and pamphlets, authored *Common Cooking* (1829) as part of *The American Frugal Housewife*. She advised combining a whole egg (shell and all) with coffee, a traditional Scandinavian practice, stirring just before the coffee was done to ensure richer and clearer coffee. Her recipe for pancakes calls for

> half a pint of milk, three great spoonfuls of sugar, one or two eggs, a teaspoonful of dissolved pearlash [an impure form of potassium carbonate and a precursor to baking powder], spiced with cinnamon, or cloves, a little salt, rose-water, or lemon-brandy. Flour should be stirred in till the spoon moves round with difficulty. If they are thin, they

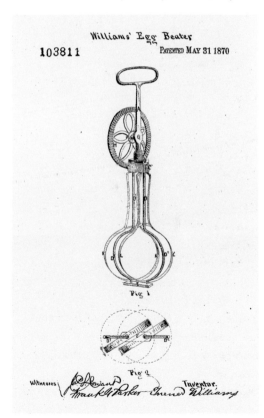

Turner Williams invented this hand-cranked egg beater in 1870.

are apt to soak fat. Have the fat in your skillet boiling hot, and drop them in with a spoon. Let them cook till thoroughly brown.[4]

Adding eight or ten eggs to a batter or dessert was commonplace, so it was fortunate that in 1870 Turner Williams invented the hand-cranked egg beater (u.s. Patent number 103,811). Its two intermeshed, counter-rotating whisks were an improvement on an earlier rotary egg beater with one whisk. A great convenience for the housewife, it was enthusiastically embraced.

German immigrants brought mayonnaise, an emulsion consisting of oil, egg, vinegar, condiments and spices, to America. Richard Hellmann opened a delicatessen in New York City in 1905, and his wife's mayonnaise recipe was featured in salads and sandwiches. It became so popular that he sold it in 'wooden boats' used for weighing butter. He put a blue ribbon around one version, which was in such high demand that in 1912 Hellmann designed what is today the iconic Blue Ribbon label, placed on glass jars. At the same time that Hellmann's Mayonnaise was flourishing in the east, Best Foods Inc. introduced mayonnaise to Californian consumers. Both brands thrived, and in 1932 Hellmann and Best Foods merged. Now both Unilever brands, today they account for about 45 per cent of all bottled mayonnaise sold in the u.s. and 72 per cent in the United Kingdom.

Mayonnaise was originally called mahonnaise, but some believe a printing mistake in an early 1841 cookbook resulted in today's spelling. Credit is given to the personal chef of Louis-Francois-Armand de Vignerot du Plessis, duc de Richelieu (1696–1788), who created the recipe to celebrate the French capture of Mahon, a city on the Spanish Isle of Minorca, in 1756. Besides enjoying a reputation as a skilful military leader, the duke was also widely known as a bon vivant with the odd habit of inviting his guests to dine in the nude. The victory feast was to include a sauce made of cream and eggs, but there was no cream in the kitchen, so the chef substituted olive oil for the cream and a new culinary creation was born, and named mahonnaise. Some food historians believe that mayonnaise, made by slowly adding oil to an egg yolk while whisking vigorously to disperse the oil, received its name from the Old French words *moyeunaise*, or *moyeu*, meaning 'egg yolk'.

From the Spanish medieval kitchen, stuffed egg recipes with different fillings found their way to Italy, France, Belgium, Britain and their colonies. Columbus Eggs appeared in 1857 in Eliza Leslie's *Miss Leslie's New Cookery Book*. During the early part of the twentieth century, Hungarians migrating to the United States brought paprika with them, which was, and still is, used to top devilled eggs, also known as stuffed and dressed eggs. From the middle of the eighteenth century 'devilled' was used to describe spicy foods, and by the late nineteenth century devilled eggs was any spiced egg preparation, stuffed or not. In America devilled eggs can be spicy or not, and even stuffed whites filled as dessert offerings fit the colloquial definition of devilled eggs. Stuffed eggs appear first in a thirteenth-century Andalusian cookbook by an anonymous author. Eggs are pounded together with cilantro (coriander), onion juice, pepper and coriander seeds, then beaten with *murri* (a condiment made from quinces, walnuts and honey), oil and salt. Once filled, the whites are fastened together with a small stick and sprinkled with pepper. During the Depression egg dishes were promoted as nutritious and economical protein sources. On 21 May 1933, President and Mrs Franklin Delano Roosevelt enjoyed stuffed eggs topped by tomato sauce as a lunch entrée at the White House. Prepared by Cornell University's Home Economics Department, it cost only seven and a half cents per serving, and the President declared it 'good'. As Richard A. Brooks, a Southern Foodways Alliance author, notes: 'Deviled eggs are eaten first – an appetizer of sorts – less from fear of microbes than the understanding that damn soon there won't be any left.'

Delmonico's restaurant, the very first public dining room opened in the U.S., is credited for Eggs Benedict. In the 1860s a regular patron, Mrs LeGrand Benedict, finding nothing to her liking on the lunch menu, asked Delmonico's chef Charles

Devilled eggs sprinkled with paprika.

Ranhofer to surprise her. Ranhofer came up with the creation, today one of the most popular brunch choices. Chef Ranhofer's cookbook *The Epicurean*, published in 1894, includes the recipe called Eggs à la Benedick (Eufs à la Benedick), misspelling her last name:

> Cut some muffins in halves crosswise, toast them without allowing to brown, then place a round of cooked ham an eighth of an inch thick and of the same diameter as the muffins one each half. Heat in a moderate oven and put a poached egg on each toast. Cover the whole with Hollandaise sauce.

Lemuel Benedict, no relation to Mrs LaGrande Benedict, contradicted the origin of the recipe in the 19 December 1942 issue of the weekly *New Yorker* magazine's 'Talk of the Town' column. He insisted that in 1894, when he was a broker on Wall Street, he went to the Waldorf Hotel in New York City

Enjoyed every day around the world, the McDonald's Egg McMuffin is a famous American contribution to the egg's past and present.

suffering from a hangover. Looking for a cure, he ordered 'some buttered toast, crisp bacon, two poached eggs, and a hooker of Hollandaise sauce'. The Waldorf's legendary chef Oscar Tschirky was so impressed that he put the dish on his breakfast and luncheon menus, substituting Canadian bacon for crisp bacon and a toasted English muffin for toasted bread. George Rector, another prominent New York restaurateur, had the last word. In his recipe for Eggs Benedict he noted that 'Good Hollandaise Sauce is undeniable proof that your husband has made a successful marriage.'

Identifying a breakfast opportunity for the restaurant chain in 1971, McDonald's franchisee Herb Peterson came up with the idea of the Egg McMuffin based on a Jack-in-the-box Eggs Benedict sandwich, which could be eaten by hand. Experimenting with pre-packaged hollandaise sauce, which he rejected as too runny, Peterson combined a slice of cheese with a hot egg, producing the perfect consistency. Since poaching eggs did not fit into the McDonald's assembly-line production process, Peterson invented a creative new cooking utensil – a cluster of six rings that was placed on the grill to shape the cooked eggs like English muffins. He complemented the egg and muffin combo with grilled Canadian bacon. The breakfast item rolled out nationally in 1975, and is today one of the most popular breakfast options in the world.

Appearing in fine-dining restaurants a few years ago, a new and very influential technique is the 'slow-cooked egg'. At first it was strange to see a translucent and almost uncooked egg as a featured course, but customers loved the culinary marvel. Chefs Viet Pham and Bowman Brown use chicken, quail or duck eggs at their Salt Lake City, Utah, restaurant Forage, and Slow Cooked Farm Egg, with soft whites and a runny yolk, is a signature dish cooked in a low-temperature water bath, a process called *sous vide*. Served in a bowl, roasted chicken broth is poured over the egg at the table, creating a new take on egg-drop soup. Another egg aficionado, chef Julian Barsotti of Nonna Restaurant in Dallas, showcases eggs in what could be called *nouveau uovo* cuisine. He tops his four-cheese-and-house-sausage white pizza with a sunny-side-up

The 'Zillion Dollar Lobster Frittata' at Le Parker Meridien, New York.

One of the famous Fabergé eggs. Only around 50 were ever made.

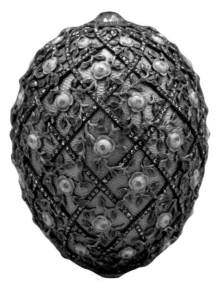

The Fabergé Rose Trellis egg.

egg. Also on his menu is *sformatino*, or little custard, of roasted cauliflower topped with a sunny-side-up egg. His ravioli includes ricotta, chard and an egg – its yolk spread enticingly over the filling. His *tajarin* is a double-egg whammy: house-made egg pasta tossed with speck (Italian smoked, cured ham) and sautéed wild rocket (arugula) crowned with two sunny-side-up quail eggs. Since bigger is better in America, Norma's Restaurant in New York's Le Parker Meridien Hotel is probably best known as the home of the 'Zillion Dollar Lobster Frittata', the world's most 'egg-spensive' omelette. This objet d'art with caviar and an entire lobster encased within its eggy folds is the creation of chef Emilio Castillo. Prepare to pay $1,000 for it, or $100 for a smaller version.

Some will spare no expense for an egg. Carl Fabergé, renowned jeweller for the Russian royal court, created a plain white enamelled egg for Tsar Alexander III to give to his wife Maria Fedorovna for Easter in 1885. To her delight, the inside contained a yolk made of gold. Inside the yolk was a golden hen, sitting on a nest of golden straw. Inside the hen was a diamond miniature of the imperial crown, concealing a tiny ruby pendant. The gift created a tradition of giving lavish eggs to commemorate milestones. For some 30 years, until 1917, when the Bolshevik Revolution began, about 50 unique imperial eggs were created, most lavishly bejewelled on the outside. They disappeared during the revolution, but continue to change hands among collectors throughout the world. Fabergé's Translucent Pink Egg sold in 2007 for U.S. $18.5 million, surely the most expensive egg ever sold.[5]

5

Bringing Eggs to Market; or, Handle with Care

Good things come in small packages.

Proverb

Agrarian societies throughout the world allowed their hens to scramble around and lay their eggs wherever it was convenient. Eggs were gathered and eaten quickly, but when American pioneers began their journey to settle the West in the 1800s, that was no longer an option. They packed their eggs in cornmeal to protect them during the long trek. Entrepreneurial travellers along the Mississippi packed their eggs in barrels of lard so they would not break, and sold both the eggs and the lard when they reached their destinations.

Both eggs and chickens underwent incredible evolutionary changes between 1850 and 1900. China loosened its restrictions on exports, opening the way for farmers to import prized Asian chicken breeds, such as the large showy Cochin, to the United States. These birds set off 'hen fever', leading to the development of breeds that laid more and better tasting eggs. Virtually every American farm started raising chickens and gathering their eggs to eat, sell or trade with neighbours. Small flocks produced the eggs, and the farmer's wife usually gathered them. Since the 'egg money'

Preserved salted duck egg.

received from selling the eggs was considered hers to keep, she often placed an egg in a nest to encourage a hen to lay there rather than in some secluded hiding place, adding to her 'nest egg', or personal stash of cash.

To keep out poachers, predators and inclement weather, farmers built outdoor poultry sheds. Challenged to increase production and get eggs to markets beyond their back yards, American ingenuity saved the day in 1818 when the Smith incubator, a large room with fans for forcing heated air to all parts of the chamber, was patented. However, it was not until 1844 that forerunners of today's efficient large-scale incubators were used to artificially hatch chicken, turkey, duck and other eggs.[1]

Petaluma, California, was to become the largest egg-production site in the world. In 1879, inventor Lyman Byce and dentist Isaac Dias invented an incubator to speed up the hatching process. Dias obtained the patent, but after his death in a hunting accident in 1884, Byce claimed the invention as his own. Byce's redwood incubators and brooders held 460–650 eggs and had a hatch rate of 90 per cent. Sales at his Petaluma Incubator Company had increased to 1,000 incubators a year by 1888. By 1917, Petaluma had shipped 16 million dozens of eggs, and the Corliss Ranch, with 50,000 chickens, was the world's largest egg farm.[2]

Before refrigerated warehousing in 1890, eggs were dry packed in bran or wood ashes and stored in a cool place, but it was expensive to transport the excess weight of the packing material. To keep eggs fresh longer, farmers sealed the pores of the shell to prevent loss of moisture. Carbon dioxide, cactus juice, soap and shellac were tried, but the most efficient was mineral oil, which is still used today. In the 1900s, water glass, a bacteria-resistant solution of sodium silicate, was used to keep eggs fresh for as long as eight to nine months. To solve a dispute between a local farmer and a hotel owner over the farmer's eggs often being delivered broken, newspaper editor Joseph Coyle of Smithers, British Columbia, invented the egg carton (or egg box, as it is known in the UK) in 1911. It was designed to carry and transport whole eggs by standing them on their ends and isolating each one in a dimpled form, twelve forms to a carton.

During the First World War, Americans were encouraged to produce more eggs to feed the troops. A circular under the direction of the State Council of Defence by the Agricultural Extension Service of the University of Wisconsin urged: 'Start a Flock. Uncle Sam's egg basket is low. Why not turn the scraps from your kitchen and the surplus from the garden into fresh eggs.' Americans rallied, and housewives compiled a war cookery book of egg recipes for the sick and wounded in 1914 to restore the strength of injured returning soldiers.[3]

Petaluma's success was guaranteed when egg prices soared from 30 to 46 cents a dozen by 1917, making the city the richest one of its size in America. Assisted by public relations expert H. W. 'Bert' Kerrigan, Petaluma took on the moniker of 'the egg basket of the world', and became so associated with chicken eggs that by the 1930s residents were called 'chickalumans'.

Backyard 'poultrymen', coined by *National Geographic* in April 1927, gradually disappeared after the war. Mechanization took over and henneries became commercialized operations. Chickens saved the day for thousands of farmers in the Midwest who suffered crop failures; after all, a 1.8 kg (4 lb) hen consuming 34–6 kg (75–80 lb) of feed could produce 30 eggs. Entrepreneurs increased flocks to 400 laying hens, which lived outside and roosted in coops, although bigger, more aggressive birds dictated a 'pecking order', eating more of the feed. Egg processing was labour intensive, and grading and inspection were done by hand. Each egg was held up to the light of a candle, called candling, for inspection, and wooden boxes were used to transport eggs to market.

New Yorker Samuel Meierfeld modified Coyle's stacking, single-sheet egg carton design by adding a lid with a label, allowing packs of six or twelve to be sold to consumers. Eggs were sold by the dozen in Britain during Elizabethan times, perhaps in honour of Jesus's twelve disciples, but from a practical packaging standpoint, it makes sense to sell eggs in even numbers. It was also discovered that eggs kept longer if they stood on their ends, so the use of cartons to package either twelve or six eggs became common.

The ability to sex chicks, or determine their gender, brought a radical change to the industry, allowing farmers to raise only the young egg-laying hens. The Japanese had long done this, but the u.s. government was unwilling to grant visas to commercial sexers. Opening a school in Vancouver, the Japanese taught Gladys Hansey the technique in the 1930s, and she

Candling eggs to check for embryos.

brought it back to Petaluma. Chickens were moved indoors and placed in trap nests so that their eggs could be identified – thus farmers bred the most prolific egg layers. Development of wire-cage battery hen houses made egg collection and clean-up easier, and allowed more chickens to be housed in smaller spaces, increasing egg production. Long hours of daylight, when chickens lay more eggs, were simulated through artificial lighting, and conveyor belts dispensed feed and collected eggs to save time and manpower.

After the Second World War, new technology resulted in conveyor belts that moved eggs to automatic washers and sorters, machines put them in cartons and refrigerated trucks delivered fresher eggs to consumers. Indoor housing led to healthier birds; productivity improved, vaccines and antibiotics reduced disease, and raised wire-floor housing and fans improved conditions for the hens. *The Egg and I* (1947), a film based on Betty McDonald's very amusing autobiography and bestselling novel, was a microstudy of the egg industry. Fred McMurray portrays a soldier returning from the war, who buys an old poultry farm and moves his new city-bred wife to the country to make his fortune. The story documents the transition of his farm from an old range house to a cage-free house; he then buys out his neighbour, who has a cage house with egg belts and the latest technology.

The Ford Motor Co., Hatcher Boaze truck used to deliver eggs, Washington, DC, *c.* 1926.

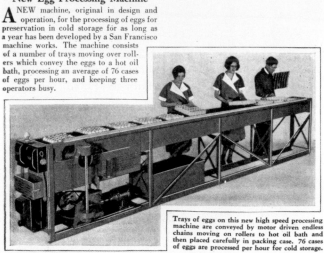

In 1931, a new egg processing machine processed 76 cases of eggs per hour, keeping three operators busy.

Flocks of 100,000 laying hens are not unusual on commercial farms in the u.s., and some flocks number more than one million birds. Each of the 235 million laying birds produces between 250 to 300 hormone-free eggs a year.

Hens lay unfertilized eggs (that is eggs laid by hens which have not mated with a rooster) in special nests or directly onto sloping floors that allow the eggs to roll onto automated conveyor belts or chutes. These modern gatherers take the eggs to refrigerated holding rooms kept at a temperature of 4–7°C (40–45°F) and a relatively high humidity. They are delivered to processing facilities with state-of-the-art computerized systems and mechanized equipment, where they are rotated, washed, sonically checked for cracks, candled over high-intensity lights, graded by standards determined by the usda, sized, packed in egg cartons and placed in shipping boxes and refrigerated trucks for delivery by robots. Millions of eggs are processed each day without being touched by human hands, and shipped the day they are laid.

Sold by size, eggs in the u.s. are labelled Jumbo, Extra Large, Large, Medium, Small and Peewee (in Europe they are labelled Very Large, Large, Medium and Small). Grading is determined by air cell, clarity of the white albumen surrounding the yolk and size. Grade AA and Grade A are sold at retail; Grade B are mostly prebroken, and sent to bakeries, food-service establishments and pasteurization plants, where the eggs are heated to a very high temperature for a second. Since 1970, when the u.s. Congress passed the Egg Products Inspection Act, all egg products distributed for consumption in America are pasteurized to destroy salmonella. Slightly more than 30 per cent of the 78 billion eggs eaten annually are processed into a liquid, frozen or dried form. Agricultural Research Service (ARS) scientists recently filed a patent on cross-flow microfiltration membrane separation, which can protect pasteurized liquid eggs from food-safety threats. More effective than thermal pasteurization at removing pathogens from liquid egg products, it does so without affecting the eggs' ability to foam, coagulate and emulsify. This means that these treated eggs could be safely substituted for pasteurized eggs in cakes and other products. Not a replacement for pasteurization, the technology works best as an accompaniment, and combining the two processes significantly reduces the danger of pathogens in speciality egg products.

Regular eggs are the most popular by a margin of 40-to-one, according to Symphony IRI, which tracks scanner data throughout the u.s. Cage-free eggs only account for 2 per cent of all retail eggs, while organic/free-range eggs account for only 1 per cent. Egg producers market more expensive speciality eggs, including vegetarian eggs, produced by hens

A modern egg factory.

Eggs lit underneath for embryo checking.

fed rations containing only vegetable foods; organic eggs, from hens fed with minimal pesticides, fungicides, herbicides and commercial fertilizers; cage-free eggs, from hens allowed to roam in barns but not outside; free-range eggs, laid by hens raised outdoors or with daily access to the outdoors; in-shell pasteurized eggs, eggs placed in warm water to kill bacteria and with shells waxed to prevent cross-contamination, ideal for hospitals, nursing homes and recipes that call for raw eggs; and nutrient-enhanced eggs, with higher levels of omega-3 fatty acids, vitamin E (a good choice for those who do not regularly eat fish) and lutein, a nutrient shown to reduce the risk of macular degeneration, the leading cause of blindness in people of 65 or older. Fertile eggs are used to manufacture many vaccines (including influenza shots), and are a source of purified protein. Although some ethnic groups consider fertile eggs a delicacy, it is comforting to know that the eggs we buy at the supermarket are non-fertile.[4]

It is fortunate for sellers that eggs are sold in sixes and by the dozen, because egg cartons are covered with more labels than any other food packaging. Labels address a multitude of consumer and industry issues, including animal welfare, food-borne illnesses and nutritional concerns. The carton can contain descriptors such as 'free-range', 'free roaming', 'veg-etarian fed' and 'cage-free', and nutrient claims for vitamin E and omega-3s. Even eggshells contain messages such as sell-by dates, or company logos stamped on each egg.[5]

Eggs bought from a food shop are already washed, san-itized and coated with a tasteless mineral oil that protects the shell. Freshness dates are important, but if you take eggs out of the carton and store them in an open egg holder in your refrigerator, do reconsider. Egg inspectors say that each time you open the refrigerator the eggs are prone to temperature fluctuations, which can help pathogens multiply to unhealthy levels. If you are unsure whether an egg is fresh, crack it open. It is fresh if the white is cloudy, but if it is pinkish-white, the egg is spoiled and should not be eaten. As the essayist, critic and author Henry James (1843–1916) noted succinctly, 'It might seem that an egg, which has succeeded in being fresh, has done all that can be reasonably expected of it.'

Salmonella Rears its Ugly Head

Worldwide, 90 per cent of the egg industry uses wire cages to house hens, but it is the most controversial practice in egg farming. Overcrowding of hens in 309–432 square cm (48–67 square in) cages is increasingly under fire, even though it keeps egg prices low. However, in the 1990s a new bacteria, *Salmonella enterica* (SE), was discovered living inside the chicken and transferring to the egg, leading to some 2.3 million SE-contaminated eggs per year, a health issue for both hens and humans. The egg industry responded to criticism by saying that the average consumer would encounter a contaminated egg only once in 84 years. One critic said that shoppers had a better chance of being in a car accident on the way to buy eggs than getting sick from eating eggs.

This was a compelling argument, perhaps, but egg sales reached all-time lows. While the industry cleaned up its barns and its image, President Bill Clinton's administration established the President's Council on Food Safety to protect Americans against food-borne illnesses, and an Egg Safety Task Force subcommittee began a plan to eliminate SE bacteria from eggs, including the addition of probotics (healthy bacteria) to feed to help make chickens more resistant to SE. In January 2002 the FDA and FSIS developed a farm-to-table food-safety strategy for eggs and egg products.

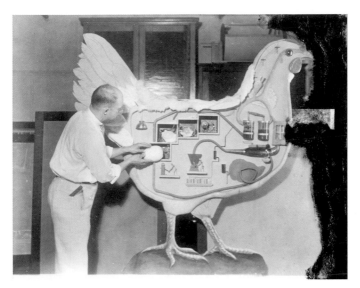
How to make eggs, 1950s.

Some consumers have become uncomfortable with the excesses of industrialization, and are willing to pay a premium for eggs laid by chickens that have room to move and dine on organic feed, docosahexaenoic acid and omega-3 fatty acids, which boost eggs' nutritional content. Smaller scale, free-range and organically fed laying flocks have made a comeback in the u.s. and Europe. Pressure to replace conventional cages offering each hen at least 432–555 sq cm (67–86 sq in) of space or more is gaining traction. There are plans for a new u.s. labelling system with four types of egg: eggs from caged hens, eggs from hens in enriched cages, eggs from cage-free hens and eggs from free-range hens. The cage system is currently being phased out in the European Union, and Swiss law now requires all hens to have free access to the outdoors.

Major food company General Mills has committed to sourcing one million eggs from hens that are not caged, and vows to use those eggs in its Häagen-Dazs ice-cream products in Europe. In the U.S. Unilever's Hellmann's Light Mayonnaise is made with cage-free eggs, and giant retailer Wal-Mart has switched to cage-free for its brand-name eggs. Quick-serve restaurant chains Burger King, Wendy's, Quiznos and CKE Restaurants followed suit, using some cage-free eggs, Subway Restaurants vows that all its eggs will soon be cage free, and although eggs at McDonald's U.S. are not cage-free, those at McDonald's Europe are.

6

Which Came First – the Chicken or the Egg?

An Egg today is better than a Hen to-morrow.
Benjamin Franklin

Christians who take the Bible literally believe that the chicken came before the egg. 'And the evening and the morning were the fourth day. And God said, "Let the waters bring forth abundantly the moving creature that hath life, and fowl that may fly above the earth in the open firmament of heaven."' (Genesis 1:19–20).

Others have different beliefs. There are many myths, legends and traditions, but it is a certainty that both birds and eggs appeared on Earth before man. A recent North Carolina State study of proteins retrieved from a 68-million-year-old *Tyrannosaurus rex* fossil confirms the long-believed evolutionary connection between dinosaurs, alligators, reptiles and today's ostriches and chickens. 'Eggs existed long before chickens did,' according to food scientist Harold McGee.

The first eggs were released, fertilized and hatched in the ocean. Around 250 million years ago, the earliest fully land-dwelling animals, the reptiles, developed a self-contained egg with a tough, leathery skin that prevented fatal water loss. The eggs of birds, animals that arose some 100 million years later, are a refined version of this reproductive adaptation to life on land. Eggs then are millions of years older than birds.[1]

Another definitive answer nests in food history. Many believe that the egg came first because when the chicken arrived in Greece and Italy in the fifth century BC, geese, ducks and guinea fowl were found laying and hatching eggs. Although these fowl eggs, which preceded chicken's eggs, were eaten, they had other uses as well. Hatched chickens were trained to fight each other to the death for the amusement of spectators, and were used in ceremonies to divine the future. The British author and poet Samuel Butler (1835–1902) was convinced that 'a chicken is just an egg's way of making another egg.' So, according to his logic, eggs existed long before chickens did. Another explanation is that a chicken is conceived and born in an egg; therefore, without the egg the chicken could not exist, a compelling argument.

'It would be hard for an egg to turn into a bird; it would be a jolly sight harder for it to learn to fly while remaining an egg,' the British scholar and author C. S. Lewis famously said. 'We are like eggs at present. And you cannot go on indefinitely being just an ordinary, decent egg. We must be hatched or go bad.' In an effort to prevent their children from 'going bad', the Mossi of Burkina Faso in Africa will not let their children eat eggs for fear that they will become thieves. The idea is not that 'he who steals an egg will steal an ox', rather 'he who steals an egg is stealing a chicken'.

To unscramble the chicken and egg debate, a team of experts, made up of Professor John Brookfield, a specialist in evolutionary genetics at the University of Nottingham, Professor David Papineau, a philosopher at King's College

Lady Gaga 'hatches' from a translucent egg to perform her song 'Born This Way' at the 53rd Grammy Awards in Los Angeles, 2011.

London, and poultry farmer Charles Bourns, deduced that the egg came first. Simply put, genetic material does not change during an animal's life. Therefore the first bird that evolved into what we would call a chicken, probably in prehistoric times, must have first existed as an embryo inside an egg. Brookfield told the UK Press Association that the pecking order is clear. The living organism inside the eggshell would have had the same DNA as the chicken it would develop into, 'Therefore, the first living thing which we could say unequivocally was a member of the species would be this first egg.' Agreeing, Papineau pointed out that the first chicken came from an egg, proving that there were chicken eggs before chickens, and added that people were mistaken if they argued that the mutant egg belonged to the 'non-chicken' bird parents. 'I would argue it is a chicken egg if it has a chicken in it,' he said. 'If a kangaroo laid an egg from which an ostrich hatched, that would surely be an ostrich egg, not a kangaroo

Hieronymus Bosch, *Concert in the Egg, c.* 1561.

Brahma, who hatched from a golden egg, at a temple in Thailand.

egg.' Bourns, firmly in the pro-egg camp, concluded, 'Eggs were around long before the first chicken arrived. Of course, they may not have been chicken eggs as we see them today, but they were eggs.'

Because of their shape, eggs embody the essence of life. People from ancient times to modern days have believed that eggs have magical qualities and the power not only to create life, but also to predict the future. Eggs, which symbolize birth, a long life and immortality, are also thought to ensure fertility. The ancients believed that the universe was hatched from an egg, called the cosmic or world egg. According to Hindu scriptures, the world began from an egg produced by a swan floating on the waters of chaos. After a year the egg split into silver and gold halves. Silver became the earth, and gold became the sky. Mountains came from the outer membrane, and clouds and mist formed from the inner membrane. Rivers rose from the veins, oceans came from the fluid within, and the sun hatched from the egg. Thus eggs represented the four elements: shell – earth; white – water; yolk – fire; and air, found under the shell at the round end of the egg.[2]

Sacred Indian writings tell of Brahma creating the continents, oceans, mountains, planets, gods, demons and humanity after bursting forth from a golden egg produced in the primeval waters by the mighty spirit of Prajapati. In the eleventh century Somadeva, an Indian poet, wrote that Shiva created the world from a drop of blood, which fell into the primeval waters. An egg was formed and out came Purusha, the Supreme Soul. Heaven and earth emerged from the two halves of his eye.

Tien, the universe's controlling power, dropped an egg from heaven to float on the waters and the first man sprang from that egg, according to the ancient Chinese. In the third century AD, an obscure Chinese work called the *San-Wu-Li-Chi* described the heaven and earth blended like the contents of an egg. Called *hun-tun*, this formation broke up after 18,000 years, creating the heavens from the bright part and the earth from the dark. In Han times, astronomical theory taught that the sphere of the heavens enclosed the earth, just as the yolk of an egg is completely enclosed by its shell. Today, when a baby is born in China the family has a red-egg-and-ginger party. New parents send a basket of red-dyed eggs to their family and friends to celebrate the birth of the child; eight or ten eggs means it is a girl, nine or eleven eggs indicates it is a boy. The invitation to the celebration party must be accepted, and giving a newborn baby an egg will bring it good fortune. Eggs are also used at Chinese burials as a symbol of life hereafter and to serve as food for the journey. The Chinese

Red-dyed eggs, which are sent to new parents in China.

consider the egg a symbol of wealth, since the yellow yolk resembles a shiny gold coin. For that reason, Chinese New Year menus include dishes that show the richness of whole, golden yolks.

According to the *Kojiki Nihonshoki*, an eighth-century Japanese history book:

> Of old, Heaven and Earth were not yet separated, and the In [Yin] and Yo [Yang] not yet divided. They formed a chaotic mass like an egg, which was of obscurely defined limits and contained germs. The purer and clearer part was thinly drawn out, and formed Heaven, while the heavier and grosser element settled down and became Earth. The finer element easily became a united body, but the consolidation of the heavy and gross element was accomplished with difficulty. Heaven was therefore formed first, and Earth was established subsequently. Thereafter divine beings were produced between them.

Hawaiians believed that a bird named Tangaroa laid the creation egg. When it broke, the sky and earth formed. Their neighbours in Samoa and the Sandwich Islands say their archipelagos formed from the shell fragments of the same egg. Samoans believed that the Samoan god Tangaloa-Langi was hatched from an egg and the Samoan islands of the South Pacific were created from scattered bits of that egg's shell. Similarly, a Finnish legend claims that Ukko, the chief god in the Finnish pantheon, sent a teal, a type of duck, to nest on Water-Mother's knee. The teal's broken golden eggs formed the earth and sky. Greenland Eskimos described the world as being like an egg, believing that the blue sky stretched above the earth, like an eggshell revolving around a high mountain far up in the north. Ancient Egyptians believed that Geb, the great cackler, and Nut, the sky goddess, produced an egg, which gave birth to the earth and sky.

According to an Italian legend, Naples was founded in 551 BC on a base of eggs. Later, Vergilius was called upon to free

These cakes with golden egg yolk inside are a traditional part of Chinese New Year menus.

it from a curse using an ostrich egg. Since the fate of the city was at stake, the egg was enclosed in a glass vessel, suspended by ribbons of silver in a cage, and sealed so that the city walls would never be violated. Vergilius warned that if ever the egg were broken, Naples would fall or sink into the sea; it was hidden in a fortress, today known as *Castrum Ovi* (Castle of the Egg). Since then, individuals in many countries have tried to protect their houses by placing eggs under them during construction. Eggshells used for this purpose have been found under houses in Holland, France, Germany, Italy and Britain.

Slava Zaitsev, a Soviet writer, proposed the theory in a 1967 article, 'Visitors from Outer Space', that ancient man may once have seen a container with a human being in it descend from the sky, emerging from a celestial egg. Of course, there has been no irrefutable evidence for this, but when one ponders the attributes of the egg, it is food for thought. Or, if you are a sceptic, this saying might apply: 'Many people are like eggs; too full of themselves to hold anything else.'

Growing up on a chicken farm, American novelist and short-story writer Sherwood Anderson (1876–1941) wondered why eggs had to be and why from the egg came the hen, which repeated the process by laying an egg. 'The question got into my blood,' he writes in the short story 'The Triumph of the Egg'.

> It has stayed there, I imagine, because I am the son of my father. At any rate, the problem remains unsolved in my mind. And that, I conclude, is but another evidence of the complete and final triumph of the egg – at least as far as my family is concerned.[3]

We will probably never know for certain which came first, but an egg is an egg is an egg, and that is enough for us to know.

7

Hatching the World from an Egg

Faith is putting all your eggs in God's basket, then counting your
blessings before they hatch.

Ramona C. Carroll

Eggs were coloured, blessed, exchanged and eaten as part of
the rites of spring long before Christian times. Even the earliest civilizations held festivals to welcome spring, the sun's rise
from its long winter sleep and proof of life's renewal. And
celebrations occur during the equinox, either of the two times
each year when the sun crosses the equator and day and night
are of equal length everywhere. During the spring (vernal)
equinox (about 21 March), it is said that an egg will stand on
its small end. Early Christian eggs were a symbol of rebirth,
and as Christianity spread the egg was adopted as a symbol
of Christ's resurrection from the tomb.

People in Central European countries have a long tradition of beautifully decorated Easter eggs. Polish and other
Slavic people create amazingly intricate designs on eggs by
drawing lines on them with a wax pencil or stylus, dipping them
in colour and repeating the process many times to make true
works of art. Traditionally, every dot and line in the pattern
can have a meaning. Yugoslavian Easter eggs bear the initials

'xv' for 'Christ is Risen', a traditional Easter greeting. During the reign of the tsars, the Russians celebrated Easter with Easter breads and other special foods, and gave gifts of decorated eggs, a tradition that continues to this day. In Germany and other Central European countries, Easter eggs are not broken, but emptied out. The empty shells are painted and decorated with bits of lace, cloth or ribbon, then hung with ribbons on an evergreen or small leafless tree. On the third Sunday before Easter, Moravian village girls carried a tree decorated with eggshells and flowers from house to house for good luck. The eggshell tree is one of several Easter traditions carried to America by German settlers, especially the Pennsylvania Dutch. They also brought the tale that the Easter bunny delivered coloured eggs for good children.

The Monday and Tuesday before Ash Wednesday, known as 'Shrovetide' from an old English word 'shrive', meaning 'to confess', is traditionally the time for 'spring cleaning', and just

Beautifully decorated Easter eggs from Central Europe.

A *beitzah* or a roasted egg appears on the Seder plate.

as houses are cleaned in preparation for Lent and the 40 days of fasting before Easter begins, so are souls through confession. Shrovetide, the last two days of 'Carnival', an unofficial period that takes its name from the Latin *carnelevare*, refers to the 'taking away of flesh' (meat) during Lent, which begins on Ash Wednesday, the day following Shrove Tuesday. Catholics want to eat while they can and get the frivolity out of their systems in preparation for the sombre Lenten period. Tuesday of Shrovetide is a particularly big party day known as 'Mardi Gras' (French for 'Fat Tuesday') – or 'Pancake Tuesday' because eggs and fats like butter in the house have to be used up before Lent. Making pancakes or waffles is traditionally a good means of using up these foods. After Lent eggs are hard-boiled, decorated and given as presents at Easter – a reward after the long fast. The Easter egg not only celebrates the end of Lenten abstinence, but also represents a Christianization of pagan egg ceremonies linking human sexuality with spring planting.

Celebrating the escape of Jewish slaves from Egypt during the reign of Pharaoh Ramses, the Jewish Passover lasts for eight days. During the first two nights friends and family come together for a ritual banquet called the Seder, which is highlighted by the Seder plate. This plate contains all the edible symbols of the Seder and is placed before the head of the household. Among the *matzahs*, shank bone and bitter herbs is a *beitzah*, or roasted egg, which is hard-cooked, then roasted in the oven until the shell becomes brown. It symbolizes the festival sacrifice made in temples in biblical Jerusalem and represents the cycle of life, renewal and fertility.

Speaking of fertility, Egyptians hung eggs in their temples to ensure it, and Nero's consort Livia was told to warm an egg on her bosom; when it hatched, the sex of the chick would foretell the sex of her unborn child. All went as predicted and the Emperor Tiberius was born, as well as the old wives' tale. Latin Americans also prized the egg as a talisman of fertility and reproduction, while French brides broke an egg when they crossed the threshold of a new home to ensure that they had many healthy children. Eggs have been on the shopping list for lovers as well. In 1907 the Kama Shastra Society published a translation by Sir Richard Burton of *The Perfumed Garden for the Soul's Delectation*, a celebrated work written by Shaykh Nafzawi recommending the consumption of particular foods as aphrodisiacs. Nafzawi insisted that

> he who boils asparagus, and then fries them in fat, and then pours upon them the yolks of eggs with pounded condiments, and eats every day of this dish, will grow very strong for coitus, and find in it a stimulant for his amorous desires.

Philippine folklore claims that man and woman hatched from the eggs of a limokon, a creature that looked like a dove and spoke like a man. The egg-hatched man, born at the mouth of the Mayo River, crossed the river one day and found a hair, which led him to the woman upstream. In a Greek myth Zeus, disguised as a swan, seduced Leda, and the heavenly twins Pollux and Castor were hatched from her eggs. Artists Leonardo da Vinci and Correggio painted the divine swan's encounter with Leda, and one of the classic poems of literary modernism is William Butler Yeats's 'Leda and the Swan'.

Egg myths are also rife half a world away in the Americas. Hatched from an egg was the Great-Coyote-Who-Was-Formed-in-the-Water of the North American Navajo. Peruvians believe that five eggs remained on a mountain-top after the creation waters receded and that the Inca hero Paricaca was born from one of them. Mayans were convinced that the egg could protect those under the spell of the evil eye. Medicine men passed an egg backwards and forwards many times before the face of a bewitched person. When the medicine man broke the egg, he looked at the yolk as though it were the evil eye and immediately buried it in a secret spot, curing the bewitched person forever of the evil spell.

It is the dependability of the rooster's early-morning call and the regularity with which newly laid eggs appear that probably inspired the Chinese to describe fowl as 'the domestic animal who knows time'. The ancient Chinese stored eggs for several years by immersing them in salt and wet clay; cooked rice, salt and lime; or salt and wood ashes mixed with a tea infusion. These eggs had greenish-grey yolks and albumen resembling brown jelly, and although the Chinese ate them with no ill effects that we are aware of, those treated eggs bore little similarity to the fresh eggs we enjoy today. The Chinese and certain tribal groups in southern Asia also used the eggs of chickens or ducks to divine the future. After painting the eggs they boiled them, and read the patterns in their cracks.

The White House Easter Egg Roll, 1929.

Oomancy was also used to predict the future by separating the white from the yolk, and pouring it into hot water to then interpret the shapes formed by the cooked egg whites.

Greeks believe eggs protect against lightening. In the Hautes-Alpes in France, the egg fights colic. A suspected sorcerer in Metz will be found out if given an egg, and in Franche-Comté France, an egg protects against a fall.

Traditionally throughout Europe, an egg laid on Good Friday or Easter day and buried in a field or garden would protect beehives. Slavic and German peasants used to smear egg on their ploughs to ensure good crops. Even today, at Easter Greeks tap red hard-boiled eggs one against the other. The last one with an unbroken egg (the trick is to protect as much of the egg as possible with your fingers) claims all the other eggs and the winner will have good luck all year.

Eggs provide merriment for people of all ages. Egg rolling on the lawn of the White House is an American tradition started by First Lady Dolley Madison in the early 1800s.[1] In England and Scotland, children roll eggs downhill and the last child with an unbroken egg is the winner. In a more complicated version of egg rolling, the players push the egg to the finishing line using only their noses. Egg races with players trying to send emptied eggshells across the finishing line by fanning them with a piece of cardboard or by blowing them are popular in Europe. Since eggs are not round, winning is not as easy as it might seem. In some English villages children still play an old game called pace egging. The name comes from *Pasch,* the word that means Easter in most European countries, and derives from *Pesach*, the Hebrew Passover. Much like Halloween trick-or-treaters, pace-eggers go from house to house in costume or with paper streamers and bright ribbons attached to their clothes. Faces blackened or masked, they sing or perform skits and demand pace eggs, either coloured hard-cooked eggs or sweets and small coins. Egg hunts are an Easter morning tradition, as children search for coloured or decorated eggs around the house or in the garden. Older children

Barack Obama at the yearly White House Easter Egg Roll, 2009.

Hens

Oops! An egg smashed on the floor;
Now the hens must lay some more.

Children's book illustration, *c.* 1950.

In Mexico, Easter is celebrated with *cascarones*, empty eggshells that are filled with *pica-pica*, or confetti.

prefer an egg toss: partners line up in two rows, face each other and each tosses a raw egg. After each hopefully successful catch, the players step further back to make the next catch more difficult, and the partners with the last unbroken egg win.

Festive *cascarones* (hollow chicken egg shells, filled with confetti) are used in Easter celebrations and fiestas in Mexico. Children bump the filled fragile eggshells on each other's heads and make a wish. If the *cascarone* breaks and showers a child with confetti, his or her wish comes true. In the sixteenth and seventeenth centuries in the Netherlands, the Egg Dance was held in taverns or at raucous rustic weddings. Performers danced all around an egg, surrounded by flowers and vegetables, situated within a chalked circle on the floor. The idea was not to break the egg, difficult enough to perform when sober, and a cause of much merriment when attempted drunk.

Peter Aaertsen, *The Egg Dance*, 1552.

Eggs provided the building blocks in seventh-century India. Monuments at Mamallapuram made use of eggs in the stucco, allowing the walls to breathe and perspire. The albumen in egg whites is a strong, coagulating, water-soluble protein used today in adhesives and varnishes. Egg whites were also used to bind church walls in the Philippines, but the yolks were thrown away. Records show that the dome of the Manila Cathedral was sealed in 1780 with a layer of lime, powdered brick, duck eggs and bamboo sap. Since millions of egg whites were used to build churches, Filipino women ingeniously began to incorporate egg yolks in their newly acquired Spanish recipes. Most of these foods, which retain their Spanish names, are still popular today.

Beauty is in the Eye of the Beholder

In medieval Russia, icon painters mixed pigment with egg emulsion by rubbing them together between their fingers into a mass, creating what is known as tempera, or egg tempera. The egg emulsion was prepared by separating the egg yolk from the white by cracking open the eggshell and catching the yolk in one hand, while allowing the white to flow through the fingers. The yolk sack was passed back and forth between the hands, drying the hand before it received the yolk. Then the sack was punctured to let the yellow flow into a dish containing distilled or boiled water – one part yolk to two parts water. One or two drops of vinegar was added to this emulsion and stirred vigorously before being added to the pigment. A good emulsion was also obtained if the water was replaced with flat beer. Icons were originally used only in religious processions and in churches. However, beginning in the fifteenth century, growing prosperity allowed for the personal ownership of icons. People placed the religious icons in their homes, either in a corner of a room or over the head of a bed. The tradition continues in many countries to this day.

'Icon' is the Greek word for an image. Icons were painted on wood using layers of egg tempera paint to create depth in colours. Figures were not represented in their natural form, but rather in their two-dimensional heavenly form with elongated proportions.

Egg yolk provided the medium to fix pigment over two millennia, adding to our enjoyment of art. Egg tempera painting dates back to the ancient Egyptians and Greeks, and was perfected by painters during the last century of the old Byzantine Empire (AD 400–1202). It flourished for about 200 years in the hands of the Early Renaissance artists, and one of the most famous examples of its use is in *La Primavera* by Sandro Botticelli in 1482. All of this beauty was made possible by the egg.[2] Renowned twentieth-century Romanian sculptor Constantin Brancusi called the egg 'the most perfect form of creation', and legend has it that he gave up sculpture because he could create nothing more perfect than the egg.

Then there is the imperfect Humpty Dumpty, one of the most iconic characters in literature, as exemplified in an illustration in Lewis Carroll's *Through the Looking Glass, and What Alice Found There*, published at Christmas in 1871. With illustrations by John Tenniel, whose anthropomorphic depiction was of a philosophical and curt personality, Humpty was shaped like a chubby egg.

The 'Humpty Dumpty' rhyme is several centuries old, with similar versions appearing in France as 'Boulle Boulle' and in Sweden as 'Lille Trille', and the term Humpty Dumpty had at least two meanings. One was as a sixteenth-century term referring to a drink made with brandy and ale, while in the seventeenth century it was used as an English slang term for a short, well-rounded and clumsy person – the type who might just fall off a wall, as in the rhyme.

> Humpty Dumpty sat on a wall.
> Humpty Dumpty had a great fall.
> All the king's horses and all the king's men
> Couldn't put Humpty together again.

Humpty Dumpty, one of the most iconic characters in literature, as exemplified in an illustration in Lewis Carroll's *Through the Looking Glass* (1871).

" I'm afraid I can't quite remember it," Alice said very politely.

" In that case we may start fresh," said Humpty Dumpty, "and it's my turn to choose a subject——" (" He talks about it just as if it was a game!" thought Alice.) " So here's a question for you. How old did you say you were? "

So was Humpty Dumpty meant to be a clumsy person, an egg or something else? There are several theories, but the most popular among folklorists and historians is that Humpty Dumpty was a large cannon used by Royalist forces to defend Colchester during the English Civil War (1642–9). The weapon, mounted on the church tower of St Mary-at-the-Wall and expertly fired by a Royalist gunner named 'One-eyed' Jack Thompson, successfully held off the Parliamentarians, or Roundheads, for eleven weeks before succumbing to a direct hit that resulted in 'a great fall' from the tower. Although the Royalists, or Cavaliers, attempted to raise Humpty Dumpty on to another part of the wall, the cannon was so heavy that the king's horses (cavalry) and king's men (infantry) could not put it together again, and the strategically important town of Colchester fell to the Parliamentarians.[3]

In *Through the Looking Glass*, Humpty says to Alice, 'When I use a word, it means just what I choose it to mean, neither more nor less.' In a slight variation, Humpty might also say: 'What am I? Whatever you choose me to be, neither more nor less.'

During rebellions 'let go my egg-o' might be an appropriate cry, when eggs were used as handy weapons. In medieval times people threw rotten eggs at their enemies and petty criminals. In eighteenth-century Britain it was common for people to hurl eggs at political and religious enemies. In 1919 crowds angrily threw rotten eggs and sang 'God Save the King' at leaders of the movement for South Africa's independence from Britain. Eggs have also been used as a verbal weapon. The Irish novelist, dramatist and critic Oscar Wilde (1854–1900) was known for his wit and sarcasm, and one of his favourite sallies to an unfeeling critic of his writing was, 'I have met a lot of hard-boiled eggs in my time, but you're twenty minutes.' One of the more memorable scenes in the Paul Newman film *Cool Hand Luke* (1967) is an egg-eating contest. Luke, a prisoner in a Southern chain gang, wagers he can eat 50 hard-boiled eggs in an hour, and accomplishes the feat after he trains to stretch his stomach and practises speed eating, not a very intelligent idea.

Throughout the world, those with high intelligence are referred to as eggheads because having a big head and high forehead are associated with being smart. Even today, new egg myths continue to arise. Egghead, a villain played by horror-film star Vincent Price was created for the 1960s *Batman* television series. The character had a pale, bald head, wore a white and yellow suit, and believed he was 'the world's smartest criminal'. His crimes usually had an egg motif to them, and he used puns such as 'egg-zactly' and 'egg-cellent'. He also used egg-shaped weapons such as laughing gas eggs and tear-gas eggs (laid by chickens fed on a diet of onions).

Vincent Price played one of Batman's freakish foes, Egghead, in the TV programme of the late 1960s.

In April 1949, Carl Barks, an author and illustrator for Walt Disney, published *Lost in the Andes*, a comic-book adventure story. In it Donald Duck and his nephews went to South America to find chickens that lay square eggs. The ducks found the square eggs, laid by square chickens, in a remote jungle and managed to escape with them. After some harrowing experiences they returned home to Duckburg exhausted and with only two chickens left (they had to eat the rest). However, they finally realized to their dismay that the entire expedition was a failure because both chickens were male and naturally could not reproduce. The comic was so popular that it caused a generation of children to ask, 'Why aren't eggs square?'

In the late 1970s, the Square Egg Co. debuted the Square Egg Press, and another company, SCI Cuisine International, introduced the Egg Cuber, inviting consumers to participate in changing the egg's natural shape; both gadgets created quite a sensation. All one had to do was take a warm hard-boiled egg, place it in the device, screw the cap down and the egg would be squared. Masashi Nakagawa, of Fukuyama, Japan, originally came up with the idea in his Apparatus for Deforming Boiled Egg, and his name is on the 1976 patent. He explained that the problem he sought to solve was that of creating ornamental boiled eggs. 'It is very troublesome and time-consuming to change the original shape by cutting it with a knife,' he writes, stating that his invention's true raison d'être was 'to

An egg cube, as produced by the Eddington's Egg Cuber.

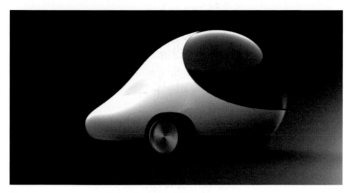
Eggy, a concept car of the future.

provide an apparatus and a method for changing a whole boiled egg into an aesthetic cubic shape.'

Eggs may not be square, but in 1989 two advertisements – 'The best square meal in the world?' and 'Try an eggsperiment', a campaign for the National Egg Coordination Committee (NEC) in Mumbai, India – won the Advertising Campaign of the Year Award of the Bombay Advertising Club.

There are also board games featuring eggs, including Lay an Egg, Egg Chess, The Happy Egg, and Don't Break the Egg, a scientific egg-drop challenge. Most recently, egg references have made their way into software. A program containing a hidden feature or novelty created by its programmers for their personal amusement – from a hidden list, hidden commands, jokes and funny animations of the developers – is called an Easter Egg.

And then there is the Eggy, a concept car of the future. Designed by Alan Gerardo Frias, it sports an elegant and eco-friendly shape that integrates the narrower part of an egg as its rear. Aside from that, the Eggy boasts a lightweight frame made of aluminum materials and emits close to no carbon dioxide. Apart from being fuel efficient because of its reduced weight, it comes with a rechargeable lithium-ion battery, and even has a red LED tail light and dark-tinted windscreen, giving drivers an exceptional driving experience.

Music aficionados may prefer eating 'music eggs'. Chickens are treated to classical, jazz, rap and Cantopop (Cantonese pop music) at the Chung Hing Musical Farm in Hong Kong's New Territories. These eggs are branded with a sticker bearing a blue treble-clef insignia with the central curl decorated to look like the head of a rooster. From the day they hatch, these fortunate chickens listen to 'age-appropriate' music, according to farmer Fong Chi-hung. Chicks up to fifteen days old listen to love songs; sixteen- to 30-day-olds are treated to fast-paced disco music. Once they are 30 days old, the music regimen becomes more flexible. When they reach twenty weeks old, the chickens enjoy music from ten to twelve in the morning, take a nap, and the music entertains them from four to six in the afternoon. The farmer believes that the music relieves stress for the chicks and makes them happier, resulting in larger yolks and better tasting eggs. He says that since he began the music regimen in 2006, the mortality of his chickens has dropped by 50 per cent. Some 500 to 600 music eggs are produced per day, and each retails for 42 Hong Kong cents.

Recipes

Libum
—*Cato's On Agriculture*, reprinted in *The Classical Cookbook*,
Andrew Dalby and Sally Grainger (1996)

Libum is an ancient Roman sacrificial cheesecake offered to household spirits during Rome's early history. The recipe below comes from the Roman consul Cato's agricultural writings, which included simple recipes for farmers. *Libum* was sometimes served hot.

Libum to be made as follows: 2 pounds cheese well crushed in a mortar; when it is well crushed, add in 1 pound bread-wheat flour or, if you want it to be lighter, just ½ a pound, to be mixed with the cheese. Add one egg and mix all together well. Make a loaf of this, with the leaves under it, and cook slowly in a hot fire under a brick.

Custarde
—from *A Propre new booke of Cokery* (London, 1545)

A custarde: the coffyn must bee firste hardened in the oven and then take a quarte of creme and five or sixes yokes of egges and beate them well together and put them into the creme and putte in suger and small reysyns and dates sliced and put into the coffyn butter or els marowe but on the fissh daies put in butter.

Egg-Pye, or Mince-Pye of Eggs
—from The Accomplish'd Lady's Delight in Preserving, Physick, Beautifying, and Cookery (London, 1675)

Take the Yolks of two dozen of Eggs hard boyled, shred them, take the same quantity of Beef-Suet, half a pound of Pippins, a pound of Currans well washt, and dry'd, half a pound of Sugar, a penny-worth of beaten Spice, a few Carraway-Seeds, a little Candyed Orange-peel shred, a little Verjuice and Rosewater; fill the Coffin, and bake it with gentle heat.

Buttered Eggs à la Martha Washington

2 anchovies
6 eggs
120 ml (½ cup) lamb gravy
¼ teaspoon salt
freshly ground black pepper
1 large tablespoon butter
grated nutmeg

Crush the anchovies with a fork and add to gravy. Beat the eggs slightly with a silver fork and add gravy to them, with salt and some pepper. Melt the butter in a skillet and add the eggs. Scramble over a slow fire. Turn on to a hot platter and grate some nutmeg over the top.

Soufflé à la Rothschild
—Marie-Antonin Carême

Created in 1829 for James and Betty de Rothschild, the richest family in France. Danziger Goldwasser is a liqueur containing suspended particles of real gold.

Soak five ounces of crystallised fruit in seven tablespoons of Danziger Goldwasser. Beat together seven ounces of pounded sugar with four egg yolks, then add three ounces of flour and two glasses of boiling milk. Bring back almost to the boil, but remove to add two whole eggs, the crystallised fruit and liqueur, and fold all into six stiffly beaten egg whites. Bake, in sugared soufflé dishes, or croustades with paper, for 25 minutes. Dust with pounded sugar five minutes before serving.

Angels Food Cake
—Ladies' Aid Society of the First Presbyterian Church of Marion, Ohio, recipe by Florence Eckhart, 1897

The whites of ten eggs, one and a half tumblers of granulated sugar, one tumbler of flour; a heaping teaspoon of cream tartar, a pinch of salt. Put through the sieve twice. Take one-half of eggs, and stir in one-half the sugar; beat until they have a gloss; then add the other half of eggs, and the rest of the sugar. Beat again; then add the flour and cream tartar. Stir up lightly. Flavor with almond. Bake one hour in slow oven.

A Rich Cake
—from Amelia Simmons's *American Cookery* (1796), the first American cookbook

Rub 2 pounds of butter into 5 pounds of flour, add 15 eggs (not much beaten) 1 pint of emptins [a mixture of hops and the dregs of beer or cider casks, an exclusively American term for a similar substance the British called 'ale yeast', 1 pint of wine

Kneed up stiff like biscuit, cover well and put by and let rise over night. To 2½ pound raisins, add 1 gill brandy, to soak over night, or if new half an hour in the morning, add them with 1 gill rosewater and 2 and half pound of loaf sugar, 1 ounce cinnamon, work well and bake as loaf cake.

Preparation des Oeufs Brouilles
—from *The Escoffier Cook Book*,
the American edition of *Guide Culinaire* (1941)

For six eggs, slightly heat one oz. of butter in a thick-bottomed saucepan. Add the six eggs, beaten moderately, together with a large pinch of salt and a little pepper; place the pan on a moderate fire, and stir constantly with a wooden spoon, taking care to avoid cooking too quickly, which, by instantaneously solidifying the egg-molecules, would cause lumps to form in the mass – a thing which, above all, should be guarded against.

When the eggs have acquired the proper consistency, and are still smooth and creamy, take the saucepan off the fire, and finish the preparation by means of one and one-half ounces of butter (divided into small quantities) and three tablespoons of cream. Only whisk the eggs to be scrambled when absolutely necessary.

Chocolate Soufflé / Mousse Cake
—courtesy of the 'Breakfast Queen' Ina Pinkney,
Ina's Restaurant, Chicago

Cake
9 eggs, large, separated
1 cup (200 g) confectioner's (icing) sugar
½ cup (50 g) cocoa powder, unsweetened
1 tsp vanilla
½ tsp cream of tartar

Preheat oven to 175°C (350°F). Line a 9" (23 cm) springform with parchment.

In a mixing bowl, combine yolks and confectioner's sugar and cocoa powder. Beat until thick and lightened in color. Add vanilla and set aside.

In a clean bowl with a clean whip, beat egg whites until frothy and large bubbles appear around the edge. Add cream of tartar and increase speed until the whites are thick and glossy. (To test, tilt the bowl. If the whites slide, they need a little more beating.) Mix a large spoonful of whites into the chocolate mixture to 'lighten" it. Gently but thoroughly fold whites and chocolate together.

Carefully pour into prepared parchment-lined springform pan. Bake at 175°C (350°F) for 35–40 minutes.

When you remove the cake from the oven, it will be a rounded cake. As it cools, the center will sink. Cool on a wire rack.

When completely cool, remove from pan by carefully loosening the edges with a metal spatula.

Filling

4 cups (1 litre) whipping cream, cold
½ cup (100 g) confectioner's (icing) sugar
¼ cup (25 g) Cocoa powder, unsweetened

Chill the bowl and beaters.

Mix all ingredients together on low speed. Scrape the bowl and increase speed. Scrape the bowl again to be sure all ingredients are mixing. Increase speed and beat until beaters leave a definite imprint in the whipped cream.

Spread filling smoothly over top and sides of cake. Decorate with chocolate shavings.

Serves 10

Mayonnaise
—reproduced by courtesy of Clifford Wright,
www.cliffordawright.com

170 ml (¾ cup) extra-virgin olive oil
170 ml (¾ cup) vegetable oil
1 large egg
1 tablespoon freshly squeezed lemon juice or good-quality white wine vinegar
½ teaspoon very fine salt
½ teaspoon very finely ground white pepper

Mix the oils together. Put the egg in a food processor and run for 30 seconds. Slowly pour in the oil in a very thin stream with the processor running, about 6 minutes of pouring. Blend in the lemon juice or vinegar for 30 seconds. Add the salt and pepper and continue blending for 30 seconds. Refrigerate for 1 hour before using. *Makes 2 cups (500 ml)*

Pound Cake

450 g (2 cups) butter
450 g (2 cups) sugar
10 eggs, separated
450 g (4½ cups) sifted flour
1 teaspoon baking powder
almond, vanilla or other flavouring

Preheat the oven to 160°c (325°F). Cream the butter until smooth and add the sugar gradually. Beat until light and fluffy. Beat the egg yolks until thick and lemon coloured. Combine with the butter and sugar mixture and beat hard until light and very fluffy. Sift together the flour and baking powder and add alternately with the stiffly beaten egg whites, beating until very smooth and light after each addition. Add the desired flavouring. Turn into two buttered and floured 20 × 20 × 8 cm (8 × 8 × 3 in) loaf pans and bake in the oven for 1½ to 1¾ hours.

Omelette Paysanne

The New York Times 60-Minute Gourmet chef Pierre Franey explained that in France, two basic methods are taught for making an omelette – à la Francesa, which is rolled and oval shaped, and à la Espanola, which is flat.

350 g (about ¾ lb) potatoes
3 tablespoons peanut, vegetable or corn oil

salt and freshly ground pepper, to taste
½ cup (80 g) halved, very thinly sliced onion
300 g (10 oz) cooked ham, cut into 1 cm (½ in) dice
4 teaspoons butter
10 eggs
1 tablespoon finely chopped parsley
1 teaspoon finely chopped tarragon
2 teaspoons finely chopped chives

Peal the potatoes and slice them as thinly as possible. Drop the slices into cold water to prevent discoloration. Drain and pat dry. Heat a skillet and add the oil. When it is very hot, add the potatoes. Do not break the slices. Sprinkle with salt and pepper. Cook, making sure that the potatoes do not stick. Brown well for about 10 minutes and add the onion. Continue cooking for about 1 minute. Add the ham and dot with 3 teaspoons of butter. Shake the skillet and gently turn over the ingredients so that they cook evenly.

Beat the eggs with a wire whisk. Add salt, pepper and herbs. Pour the eggs over the ham and potato mixture. Gently stir the mixture from the bottom, allowing the egg mixture to flow to the bottom. Cook over a high heat. Lift up the edges of the omelette and let the remaining butter flow beneath the omelette. Shake the skillet to make certain that the omelette is loose. Place a large plate over the skillet and quickly invert the skillet, letting the omelette fall into the plate. This omelette is best served hot, but it is also delicious at room temperature.

Yields 4 servings

The Devil Made Me Do It

A classic recipe for devilled eggs is simple but divine. Cut a dozen hard-cooked chicken eggs in half lengthways or across, scrape out the yolks and mash them with a fork. Add 120 ml (½ cup) mayonnaise, 2 teaspoons yellow mustard, garlic salt, onion and / or shallot to taste, pepper, a dash of vinegar and sugar. Spoon the spreadable mixture back into the whites and sprinkle with paprika.

For those who like to experiment with flavour, chop and mix any of these into the filling: bacon, cheese, corned beef, cucumber, cumin, dill or tarragon, cooked lobster, peanuts, pickle relish, pine nuts, radish, watercress, barbecue sauce, blue cheese, chipotle, curry powder, cream cheese, sour cream, crème fraiche, dashi flakes, French onion dip, guacamole, humus, lemon or lime zest, pesto sauce, salsa, truffle oil, wasabi, or Worcestershire or Tabasco sauce. To garnish use shrimp, alfalfa or radish sprouts, anchovies, capers, caviar, cornichones or gherkins, giardiniera, microgreens, nori, olives, smoked salmon, smoked paprika, truffles, or Za'atar or sumac.

Hoppelpoppel

Hoppelpoppel, a speciality of Berlin, Germany, is an excellent recipe for using leftovers for breakfast. In this dish bacon (or other meat) is cut into pieces, then scrambled together with eggs, potatoes, onions and seasonings. It is easy to make and delicious.

The word 'hoppelpoppel' is taken from an old children's poem called 'Pottkieker' (the person who peeked into the pot), according to Jillian-Beth Stamos-Kaschke of Berlin. The poem goes, 'Mummy, mummy, what's in the pot?' to which the mother rather impolitely replies, 'Hoppel, Poppel, Appelreis, mach' dich fort, Naseweis' (hoppel, poppel, apple rice, now get lost, nosy child). Hoppel Poppel is also a form of eggnog, prescribed to soothe a sore throat.

4 egg yolks
120 ml (½ cup) honey
100 g (3½ oz) sugar
1 teaspoon vanilla
700 ml (3 cups) hot milk
240 ml (1 cup) light (single) cream
240 ml (1 cup) brandy
cinnamon or nutmeg, for dusting
pat of butter, if desired

Beat the egg yolks with the honey and sugar to sweeten. Add the vanilla. Slowly pour in the hot milk mixed with the cream. Add the brandy. Heat thoroughly on the stove and pour into pre-warmed mugs. Dust with cinnamon or nutmeg, and add a pat of butter if desired.

Serves 6

Mama Mary's Potato Salad

3 white potatoes
4 eggs
1 small onion
1 teaspoon salt
½ bottle Miracle Whip, or 425g Heinz Salad Cream
1 teaspoon mustard
1 teaspoon pickle relish
115 g (4 oz) whipping cream

Bring the potatoes, with the skins left on, to the boil over a lower heat, then simmer until hard cooked. Meanwhile hard-boil the eggs and let both cool. Peel the potatoes and cut them into small pieces. Peel the onion and cut it into small pieces, then mix with the potatoes. Cut the eggs into pieces and add to the potato and onion mix. Add salt. In a separate bowl, make the dressing with the Miracle Whip, mustard, pickle relish and cream. Fold the dressing into the potato mixture. Refrigerate for an hour before serving.

Marshall Field's Recipe for Rich Scones

At the turn of the century Marshall Field's Department Store in Chicago, Illinois, served tea to its wasp-waisted, picture-hatted customers as they relaxed after shopping or met with friends. In 1986 Marshall Field's Traditional Tea at Three was modelled after the famous High Tea at the Hyatt Carlton Tower, London.

Pastries and scones were prepared under the direction of Robert Mey, renowned chef patissier of the Hyatt Carlton Tower.

225 g (8 oz) plain flour
15 g (½ oz) baking powder
60 g (2 oz) butter
1 egg
4 ounces (120 ml) milk
60 g (2 oz) caster sugar
60 g (2 oz) currants or sultanas

Preheat the oven to 230°C (450°F). Sift together the flour and baking powder. Cut in the butter. Add the egg and milk to make a soft dough consistency. Mix in the sugar and fruits, and roll out the dough to 1 cm (½ inch) thickness. Cut into rounds. Arrange on a greased baking tray. Brush the tops with beaten egg or milk. Bake for 15 minutes. Allow to cool. Serve with butter, clotted cream and jam.

Waffles

Juliette Gordon Low was the founder of the Girl Scouts of America in 1912. This was her secret recipe for waffles, which she cooked on her electric waffle iron. It was provided by Daisy Gordon Lawrence, her niece, namesake and the first registered Girl Scout.

2 cups (250 g) flour
1 teaspoon sugar
1 teaspoon salt
480 ml (1 pint) milk
60 ml (½ cup) salad oil
3 eggs
3 rounded teaspoons baking powder

Sift together the flour, sugar and salt, pour in the milk and beat until smooth. Add the salad oil and well-beaten eggs. Last of all, add the baking powder. Brush a preheated waffle iron with melted butter. Pour mix onto hot waffle iron. Cook until golden brown on each side and serve hot.

Yields 8 waffles

Original Nestlé Toll House Cookies

270 g (2¼ cups) all-purpose (plain) flour
1 teaspoon baking soda
1 teaspoon salt
225 g (1 cup) butter, softened
50 g (¼ cup) sugar
45 g (¼ cup) firmly packed brown sugar
1 teaspoon vanilla extract
2 eggs
1 12-ounce (340 g) package Nestle Toll House semi-sweet morsels, or other chocolate chips
120g (4¼ oz) 1 cup chopped nuts

Preheat the oven to 190°C (375°F) In a small bowl, combine the flour, baking soda and salt; set aside. In a large bowl, combine the butter, sugars and vanilla extract; beat until creamy. Beat in the eggs. Gradually add the flour mixture. Stir in Nestle Toll House Semi-sweet chocolate morsels and nuts. Drop rounded tablespoonfuls of the mixture onto an ungreased baking tray. Bake for 9–11 minutes.

Makes 5 dozen 6¾ cm (2¼ inch) cookies

Full of Hot Air – Vegetable Soufflé
—Judith Dunbar Hines, Director of Culinary Arts and Events
for the Chicago Department of Cultural Affairs

Soufflé is a French word meaning 'puffed up'. Adding each egg separately to this dish allows air to be incorporated for a puffed up result. Most home cooks are intimidated by the idea of preparing a soufflé. Oh, the embarrassment during a dinner party as they open the oven to find flattened, inverted scrambled eggs. Professional chefs enjoy perpetuating the myth that only they can make soufflés, but the truth is that there are tricks to ensure a successful result.

Use older eggs, which whip up higher than fresh ones. To combine the ingredients, add the light ones to the heavy ones one-third at a time; spoon gently around the edge and through the middle of the bowl, and turn or flip over the ingredients. Do not open the oven door more than once, and make it quick. Most important, if the roux (a mixture of butter and flour) is cooked to the proper stage, the soufflé will turn out perfectly – cook it until it begins to smell like burning grain.

1 cup cooked vegetables. You can use broccoli, courgettes, asparagus, carrot, tomato, Romaine lettuce and tomato or cauliflower
3 tablespoons butter
4 tablespoons flour
240 ml (1 cup) milk
6 egg yolks
salt and pepper
nutmeg
8 egg whites
⅛ teaspoon cream of tartar
¾ cup (90 g) Swiss cheese
¼ cup (30 g) Parmesan cheese

Preheat the oven to 200°C (400°F) Butter a soufflé dish and sprinkle it with the Parmesan cheese. Make a collar of aluminium foil which rises halfway over the top of the dish, wrap it around the outside and tie with string.

Cook the vegetable you are using, drain well and dice into small pieces. Make a roux by melting the butter over a low heat, whisking in the flour and cooking it until it starts to smell like burned or toasted grain. Add the milk and form a thick sauce by whisking constantly over a medium heat. Let cool. Add the yolks one at a time, beating after each addition. Add the vegetable, cheese, seasoning and nutmeg. Beat the egg whites with the cream of tartar until very stiff.

Fold the vegetable mixture into the whites in two steps only – they do not need to be completely mixed. Fill the pre-prepared soufflé dish with the mixture. Sprinkle the top of the dish with cheese. Place in the oven and lower the heat immediately to 190°C (375°F). Bake for 25 minutes. Serve immediately with Mornay sauce on the side.

Mornay Sauce
1 tablespoon butter
1 tablespoon flour
240 ml (1 cup) milk
3 tablespoons grated Swiss cheese
1 tablespoon Parmesan cheese
1 teaspoon Dijon-style mustard
1 tablespoon chopped tomato, optional

Make a roux as in the previous recipe, and add the cheese and mustard after the sauce has thickened (for colour, you can add a tablespoon of chopped tomato).
Makes 6 to 8 portions

Crème Brûlée
—adapted from *Saveur* magazine, No. 148

1 litre (2 pints) heavy (double) cream
1 vanilla bean, halved lengthways, seeds scraped and reserved
150 g (¾ cup) sugar
8 egg yolks
demerara or turbinado sugar, for serving

Preheat the oven to 150°C (300°F). Bring the cream and vanilla bean with the seeds to a simmer in a 2 litre (4 pint) saucepan over a medium-high heat. Remove from the heat and let sit for 30 minutes; discard the vanilla bean. In a bowl, whisk the sugar and yolks until smooth. Slowly pour in the cream mixture, whisking until smooth; set aside.

Place a paper towel in the bottom of a 25 x 35 cm (9 x 13 in) baking pan, and place six 170 g (6 oz) ramekins inside the pan. Divide the custard among the ramekins. Pour boiling water into the pan to come halfway up the outsides of the ramekins. Bake until the custards have set but are still slightly loose in the centre, about 35 minutes. Transfer the ramekins to a wire rack; cool. Chill until firm, at least four hours.

Dab any condensation off the surfaces of the custards with a paper towel. Sprinkle the demerara sugar evenly over the surface of each custard. Guide the flame of a blowtorch back and forth over each surface until the sugar caramelizes; let sit briefly until the sugar hardens.

Serves 6

Julia Child's Hollandaise Sauce

This classic recipe is adapted from the TV series
Julia and Jacques Cooking at Home

3 egg yolks
1 tablespoon water
1 tablespoon fresh lemon juice, if needed (or more)
170–225 g (6–8 oz) very soft unsalted butter
salt, to taste
freshly ground white pepper, to taste
dash of cayenne pepper

Whisk the yolks, water and lemon juice in a saucepan for a few moments, until thick and pale (this prepares them for what is to come). Set the pan over a moderately low heat and continue to whisk at a reasonable speed, reaching all over the bottom and insides of the pan, where the eggs tend to overcook. To moderate the heat, frequently move the pan off the burner for a few seconds, then back on. (If, by chance, the eggs seem to be cooking too fast, set the pan in a bowl of cold water to cool the bottom, then continue.)

As they cook, the eggs become frothy and increase in volume, then thicken. When you can see the pan bottom through the streaks of the whisk and the eggs are thick and smooth, remove from the heat. By spoonfuls, add the soft butter, whisking constantly to incorporate each addition. As the emulsion forms, you may add the butter in slightly larger amounts, always whisking until fully absorbed. Continue incorporating butter until the sauce has thickened to the consistency you want. Season lightly with salt, pepper and a dash of cayenne pepper, whisking in well. Taste and adjust the seasoning, adding droplets of lemon juice if needed. Serve lukewarm.

Makes 1.5 cups (350 ml)

Egg Lemon Soup (Avgolemono)

1½ litres (2 pints) chicken stock
1½ cups (310 g) orzo
1 egg
3 egg yolks
juice of 2 lemons, or more
salt and pepper, to taste

Heat the stock in a saucepan, add the orzo, cover and simmer 20 minutes.

Beat the whole egg and yolks constantly until light, while slowly adding the lemon juice. Measure 450 ml (1 pint) hot chicken stock and add tablespoon by tablespoon to the egg mixture, beating constantly to prevent curdling. Add this mixture to the remaining hot chicken stock with the orzo, and season with salt and pepper. Serve at once.

Serves 6

French Macaroons
—courtesy of chef Chris Hanmer, owner of the School of Pastry Design, Las Vegas. In 2004 Chris became the youngest American to win the title of World Pastry Champion.

300 g (10 oz) almond flour
300 g (10 oz) icing sugar
food colours
110 g (4 oz) egg whites
300 g (10 oz) granulated sugar
75 ml water
110 g (4 oz) egg whites

Preheat the oven to 150°C (300°F). Sift together the almond flour and icing sugar. Stir the colour into the first half of the egg whites. Pour them over the mixture of icing sugar and almond flour and mix to a paste.

Bring the water and granulated sugar to a boil and cook to 118°C (245°F). When the syrup reaches 115°C (240°F), start whisking the second half of the egg whites to soft peaks on a medium speed. When the sugar reaches 118°C (245°F), pour it over the egg whites. Whisk and allow the meringue to cool down to 50°C (122°F), then fold it into the almond-sugar mixture. Spoon this batter into a piping bag with a plain nozzle. Pipe quarter-sized rounds of batter on a Silpat baking mat. Tap the tray on the work surface covered with a kitchen cloth. Let stand for at least 30 minutes until a skin forms on the shells. Bake for 10 to 12 minutes.

French Butter Cream Filling

450 g (15 oz) granulated sugar
130 g (4½ oz) glucose
85 ml water
130 grams whole eggs
77 grams egg yolks
770 g (25 oz) softened unsalted butter

Cook the sugar, glucose and water to 118°C (245°F). In a stand mixer fitted with a whisk, mix the whole eggs and yolks until light. Slowly pour the hot syrup into the egg mixture. When the mixture is cool, add the soft butter to the egg mixture a piece at a time. When all the butter is mixed in add any flavouring and / or colouring you like.

References

Introduction: Walking on Eggs

1 Martin Yan, *Martin Yan's Culinary Journey through China* (San Francisco, CA, 1995), p. 58.
2 Harold McGee, *On Food and Cooking* (New York, 2004), pp. 84–117.
3 Select Committee on Nutrition and Human Needs, U.S. Senate, 'Dietary Goals for the United States' (Washington, DC, 1977).
4 Public Law 101–445, Title III, 7 USC 5301 et seq.
5 USDA, 'Dairy and Egg Products', www.ars.usda.gov/nutrientdata, accessed 29 August 2013.
6 American Egg Board, *The Incredible Edible Egg: Eggcyclopedia* (Park Ridge, IL, 1999).
7 'Medicine: The Egg and He', *Time* (May 1946).

1 What Is More Perfect than an Egg?

1 Urbain de Vandenesse, 'Egg White', *The Encyclopedia of Diderot et d'Alembert*, Collaborative Translation Project, trans. A. Wendler Uhteg, University of Michigan Library (Ann Arbor, MI, 2011). Originally published as 'Blanc d'oeuf', *Encyclopédie ou Dictionnaire raisonné des sciences, des*

arts et des métiers (Paris, 1752), vol. II, p. 272.

2 Ibid.

3 John Ayto, *An A–Z of Food and Drink* (Oxford and New York, 2002), p. 117.

4 Isabella Beeton, *Mrs Beeton's Book of Household Management*, 3rd edn (New York, 1977), p. 823.

5 Dal Stivens, *The Incredible Egg: A Billion Year Journey* (New York, 1974), p. 318.

6 Gareth Huw Davies, 'The Life of Birds: Parenthood', www.pbs.org/lifeofbirds, accessed 28 August 2013.

7 Ian Phillips, 'The Man Who Unboiled an Egg', *The Observer* (19 February 2010).

8 Kent Steinriede, 'Food, With a Side of Science', *Scientist Magazine*, Ontario (July 2012).

9 Philip Dowell and Adrian Bailey, *Cooks' Ingredients* (New York, 1980), p. 236.

2 The History of Eggs

1 Kenneth F. Kiple and Kreimhild C. Ornelas, *Cambridge World History of Food* (Cambridge, 2000), vol. I, p. 499.

2 Joe G. Berry, 'Artificial Incubation', www.thepoultrysite.com, 15 April 2009.

3 Maguelonne Toussaint-Samat, *History of Food*, trans. Anthea Bell (New York, 1992), p. 356.

4 H. Thurston, 'Lent In', *The Catholic Encyclopedia* (New York, 1910), www.newadvent.org.

5 D. Allen, *Irish Traditional Cooking*, ed. K. Cathie (London, 1998), p. 118.

6 Mairtin Mac Con Iomaire and Andrea Cully, 'The History of Eggs in Irish Cuisine and Culture', in *Proceedings of the Oxford Symposium on Food and Cookery 2006*, ed. Richard Hosking (London, 2007), pp. 137–47.

7 Naomichi Ishige, 'Eggs and the Japanese', in *Proceedings of the Oxford Symposium on Food and Cookery 2006*, ed. Hosking, p. 104.

8 Charles Perry, 'Moorish Ovomania', in *Proceedings of the Oxford Symposium on Food and Cookery 2006*, ed. Hosking, pp. 100–06.

9 Clifford A. Wright, *A Mediterranean Feast* (New York, 1999), p. 136.

10 Ken Albala, 'Ovophilia in Renaissance Cuisine', in *Proceedings of the Oxford Symposium on Food and Cookery 2006*, ed. Hosking, pp. 11–19.

11 Reay Tannahill, *Food in History* (New York, 1973), pp. 82, 83, 93, 94, 113, 174, 175, 283.

12 Ibid.

13 G. Gershenson, 'Crème de la Crème', *Saveur*, CXLVIII (2012), p. 46.

14 Ian Kelley, *Cooking for Kings: The Life of Antonin Careme, the First Celebrity Chef* (New York, 2003).

3 No Eggs, No Cuisine

1 Global Industry Analysts Inc., 'Eggs: A Global Strategic Business Report' (San José, CA, 2010).

2 Karen Hursh Graber, 'Eggs: A Mexican Staple from Soup to Dessert' (2008), at www.mexconnect.com.

4 Eggs in American Cuisine

1 Marie Kimball, *The Martha Washington Cook Book* (New York, 1940), pp. 43–4.

2 Florence Eckhart, 'Recipes Tried and True', Ladies' Aid Society of the First Presbyterian Church of Marion, Ohio (1897), Project Gutenberg, www.gutenberg.net.

3 Yvan D. Lemoine, *Food Fest 365!* (Avon, MA, 2010), p. 293.

4 Noel Rae, ed., *Witnessing America: The Library of Congress Book of Firsthand Accounts of Life in America, 1600–1900* (New York, 1996), pp. 274, 292, 293, 294, 295.

5 Parmy Olson, 'Fabergé Egg Goes Back to Its Nest', *Forbes* (November 2007).

5 Bringing Eggs to Market; or, Handle with Care

1 Andrew F. Smith, ed., *The Oxford Encyclopedia of Food and Drink in America* (New York, 2004), vol. 1, pp. 425–8.
2 Ibid.
3 Jessie M. Laurie, *A War Cookery Book for the Sick and Wounded: Compiled from the Cookery Books by Mrs. Edwards, Miss May Little, etc., etc.* (London, 1914), pp. 16–18, http://digital.library.wisc.edu.
4 Kimberly L. Stewart, *Eating Between the Lines* (New York, 2007), pp. 73–94.
5 Ibid.

6 Which Came First – the Chicken or the Egg?

1 Harold McGee, *On Food and Cooking* (New York, 2004), pp. 69–70.
2 Venetia Newall, *An Egg at Easter: A Folklore Study* (Bloomington, IN, 1971).
3 Sherwood Anderson, *Triumph of the Egg: A Book of Impressions from American Life in Tales and Poems* (New York, 1921).

7 Hatching the World from an Egg

1 Anna Barrows, *Eggs: Facts and Fancies About Them* (Boston, MA, 1890).
2 The Art of the Egg', at http://madsilence.wordpress.com (2007).

3 Ben Macintyre, 'Gory Reality Behind Nursery Rhymes', *The Times*, London (30 August 2008).

Select Bibliography

Andrews, Tamra, *Nectar and Ambrosia: An Encyclopedia of Food in World Mythology* (Santa Barbara, CA, 2000)

Derbyshire, David, 'Poisoned Food in Shops for Three Weeks: Supermarkets Clear Shelves of Cakes and Quiches Containing Contaminated Eggs from Germany', *Daily Mail* (8 January 2011)

Dias, Elizabeth, 'A Brief History of Eggnog', *Time* (21 December 2011)

Flandrin, Jean-Louis, and Massimo Montanari, eds, *Food. A Culinary History*, trans. Albert Sonnenfield (New York, 1999)

Leake, Christopher, 'EU to Ban Selling Eggs by the Dozen: Shopkeepers' Fury as They are Told All Food Must Be Weighed and Sold by the Kilo', *Daily Mail* (15 August 2012).

Levy, Glen, 'Did Lady Gaga Really Stay Inside the Egg for 72 Hours?', *Time* (16 February 2011)

Jull, M. A., 'The Races of Domestic Fowl', *National Geographic* (April 1927)

Katz, Solomon H., and William Ways Weaver, eds, *Encyclopedia of Food and Culture*, vol. 1 (New York, 2003)

Melish, John, *Travels in the United States of America in the Years 1806 & 1807, and 1809, 1810 & 1811* (Philadelphia, PA, 1812)

Pinkard, Susan, *A Revolution in Taste: The Rise of French Cuisine, 1650–1800* (New York, 2009)

Smith, Andrew F., ed., *The Oxford Companion to American Food and Drink* (New York, 2007)

Trager, James, *The Food Chronology* (New York, 1995)

Wilson, Anne, *Food and Drink in Britain: From the Stone Age to the 19th Century* (Chicago, IL, 1991)

Yalung, Brian, 'Eggy Egg-Shaped Concept Car', *TFTS* (4 June 2010)

Associations and Websites

Associations

American Egg Board
www.aeb.org

British Egg Products Association
www.bepa.org.uk

Egg Farmers of Canada
http://eggs.ca

Egg Farmers of Ontario
www.eggfarmersofontario.ca

Egg Nutrition Center
www.eggnutritioncenter.org)

International Poultry Council
www.internationalpoultrycouncil.org

Pacific Egg and Poultry Association
www.pacificegg.org

United Egg Producers
www.unitedegg.org

u.s. Poultry & Egg Association
www.uspoultry.org

Egg Culinary History

Clifford Wright
(Clifford Wright is one of the most knowledgeable food history
and culinary experts)
www.cliffordawright.com

Epicurious
www.epicurious.com

History of Eggnog
whatscookingamerica.neteggnog.htm

History of Eggs Benedict
whatscookingamerica.net/history/eggbenedicthistory

History of Sauces
whatscookingamerica.net/history/saucehistory

Uses of Eggs Worldwide
Smithsonian
blogs.smithsonianmag.com/food/2010/05/
around-the-world-in-80-eggs

Zester Daily
(American food and wine online magazine)
www.zesterdaily.com

Photo Acknowledgements

The author and the publishers wish to express their thanks to the below sources of illustrative material and/or permission to reproduce it.

© The Trustees of the British Museum, London: p. 115; Corbis: p. 97 (Lucy Nicholson/Reuters); Dreamstime: pp. 22 (Vasiliy Vish-nevskiy), 47 (Akinshin), 62 (Tanyae), 106 (Photowitch); Evan-Amos: p. 78; A. Gerado: p. 121; Ischai: p. 42; iStockphoto: pp. 66 (violettenlandungoy), 74 (craftvision), 77 (LeeAnn White), 107 (stirling_photo); Komnualtså: p. 30; Library of Congress, Washington, DC: pp. 93, 110; Lusifi: p. 113; National Archives, Washington, DC: pp. 12, 57; National Gallery of Art, Washington, DC: p. 20; National Library of Medicine, Bethseda: p. 8; Isabelle Palatin: p. 9; Pengrin: p. 102; Raul654: p. 29; Rex Features: pp. 79 (Sipa Press), 119 (c/20th Century Fox/Everett); Shutterstock: pp. 6 (Miguel Garcia Saavedra), 11 (Rob Byron), 15 (Sea Wave), 24 (gururugu), 34 (Stubblefield Photography), 39 (margouillat photo), 53 (Lesya Dolyuk), 64 (tommaso lizzui), 65 (Lilyana Vynogradova), 80 top left (Shevchenko Nataliya), 83 (apple2499), 90 top (nikkytok), 100 (KobchaiMa), 103 (jreika); stu_spivack: p. 61; Thinkstock: p. 90 bottom (iStockphoto); UK College of Agriculture, Food and Envionment: p. 86; United States Patent and Trademark Office: p. 73; V&A Museum, London: p. 52; Walters Art Museum, Baltimore: p. 80 bottom centre; The White House: p. 111 (Pete Souza).

Index